Rhea Powers

A Call to the Lightworkers

Dedication:

This book is dedicated to my teachers both in and out of form.

A Call
to the Lightworkers

BY

RHEA POWERS

all design Verlag

©   German Version:
      by CH.-Falk-Verlag, Seon
      ISBN 3-924161-06-2

©   English Version:
      all design Verlag Stuttgart, Germany 1990

1. edition   Sept. 1990 0 - 2000
2. edition   Dec.   1991 2001 - 4000
3. edition   Dec.   1993 4001 - 7000

Cover design: Alois Hanslian
Photo of Rhea Powers by Lilan Gilden

Printing: RR Donnelley & Sons Company
Printed in the USA
ISBN 3-928006-00-2

Foreword

I began what is now popularly called channeling, rather by accident, in July of 1983. During one of my first experimental sessions I was asked to bring through a book by a transpersonal aspect of consciousness that identified itself as the ascended master, Sanat Kumara. I agreed. This is the book.

Starting on September 1, 1983, and continuing for six weeks, I went into trance each morning at 7:00 (regardless of what time zone I was in) and turned on the tape recorder and began speaking. The sessions usually lasted twenty to thirty minutes. I transcribed them on a word processor verbatim. I found the book so profound and poetic that, to date, I have not changed a word of it. The chapter divisions were given as, in most cases, were the sentence and paragraph breaks.

The Venus mentioned in the book is not the Venus you would see through a telescope. In my understanding, it is a symbol for a state of consciousness.

Through the years my experience of channeling has evolved. I now see it as connecting with a transpersonal aspect of consciousness -- not to Beings that are separate from who I am but to a realm of awareness that is beyond my personal identity. And still, even with that understanding, I can not explain this book. Often a session would end in the middle of a paragraph and the next day the channeling began with the next sentence in the paragraph. It was as if it was already written and was simply being read to/through me. Though my own understanding has evolved over the years, this book continues to touch me. It is my hope that it also touches you.

Rhea Powers
P. O. Box 6546
Santa Fe, NM 87505

CHAPTER ONE

Imagine nothing. Imagine everything. Neither of these can be held purely in the imagination. So, imagine a ball, a sphere of perfect light, perfect harmony, pure energy. Imagine that that is all that there is. It is at once everything and nothing. Being everything there can be nothing else.

In nothingness there is no time, no form, no space, no distance. There only is Isness. In Isness there is no experience, even of oneself. That is to say, the Isness cannot experience itself because it is all that there is and there is nothing to reflect it, nothing to delineate it. Isness, God, if you choose to call it that, in order to experience itself, split into millions, and millions, and millions of parts of itself. Each of those parts may be imagined as a spark, a hologram of the whole, reflecting all and yet defining separateness. And in the separateness the Is can experience itself. It can come to know itself. It can play a game. The game that it created includes Earth. It includes myriads of other physical realities, and myriads and myriads and myriads of non-physical realities, frequently called in some disciplines, bardos, other realms of consciousness, spheres of creation beyond the normal physical terms.

Each of the parts of the Isness, each of these sparks, in order to know itself, chose games to play, chose ways to come to know itself. Earth is a manifestation. The Earth itself is a spark. It in itself has consciousness. It in itself has form. All the planets do. All physical reality does. Everything does, because that is all that there is, ultimate Isness.

Some of the sparks express themselves as human souls. Human souls are attached to the planet Earth. You, reading this book, have chosen to express your own self, your own Isness, as a human being, a human consciousness and a human form existing on the planet Earth. You choose to come here. This is the place that you choose to express and manifest yourself in your own game. You're creating this reality now.

In this reality there are many, many levels of awareness. It is the intention of this book to open your awareness to another level, to a level beyond the one that you are experiencing as you read these words. By the end of the book, that awareness, the awareness within your own self, will have expanded to include a multi-dimensional expression of what you call Truth, of ultimate reality.

In the game humans choose to play, there was once upon a time a place called Earth. Time, distance and form are all relative to the human experience on the planet Earth. Each of these is perceived by the individual human being in its own unique fashion. Which is to say, your perception of your reality can never, ever be matched, experienced, or expressed by another's. That is the joy of the myriad and millions and millions of sparks. Each of them reflects and contributes to each other. So that while you can discover parts of yourself, parts of your self in all other physical presences and maybe even non-physical presences, those sparks that you define as not you are actually parts of you reflecting parts of you that you cannot see in any other way but through their reflection. Those reflections contribute to your experience of who you are and in absorbing that reflection you are then enlarged and expanded and able to express more fully the myriad, multi-dimensional potential that is yours for the claiming.

In the game human beings are playing on Earth, there is a cloud, a cloud of suffering, a cloud of pain, a cloud of fear surrounding the human experience. That suffering, that pain, and that fear has reached a critical point. A point where a shift is necessary. The shift has been referred to as a shift in axis, that is to say in polarity, the polarity between good and evil. The basic duality created by the human mind, thought necessary to experience good, which is to say, within the human system it was believed that in order to experience God, or good (if you want to put another "o" in it) it was necessary to experience evil. It was necessary to reverse life. It has been pointed out many times that evil is live spelled backward, and it is a reversal of the true purpose of life that has brought about evil in human experience of the planet Earth. The true purpose of life, of form, of space, of individual consciousnesses is joy, celebration and a rejoicing in all that is possible in all dimensions.

In the human mind the need for duality has presenced itself with good and evil. Fear, suffering and pain all come under the pole called evil. It is not necessary to experience evil in order to know good. The shift in axis that has been long prophesied for the planet Earth is actually a shift in polarity, that is to say a moving away from duality, a moving away from the supposed need to experience and indeed, create as humans have created evil in order to experience good or God. That shift is approaching very, very rapidly.

If the consciousness of the planet is raised, and the potential is there and is now being manifested in many, many forms and in many, many systems on the planet, if that shift is made and humans abandon the desire for evil in the misinterpreted hope that they could then experience good, there will be no destruction, there will be no disaster, there will be no holocaust, there will be no Armagedon, there will be no rapter. However, it is a choice that each individual spark must make. It is very true that if a large balance of the sparks, or souls, or consciousnesses on this planet choose to abandon the pole referred to as evil, then that destruction will be averted. It is the purpose of this book to allow you to consciously make that choice, to con- front and face that choice within yourself, and to move you forward toward God.

There are many, many systems of thought that have been promul- gated on this planet. There are many systems of religion, philosophy, psychology, folklore that have shaped your point of view. We ask that you listen to the words that you are reading beyond these systems, that you rise above the customary filter of your experience and allow that part of you which is deeper within the core of your being to hear the truth as you read.

So if you are a Catholic, for a moment we ask you to experience your true Catholicism, the universality of goodness. If you are Buddhist we ask you to allow the compassion of Buddha to spread open your heart, and allow you to hear the truth of these words. If you are Confucian, we ask you to set aside the system which would deline- ate your experience and allow you, as Confucious did, to listen to your own heart. We ask you to set aside whatever systems you generally perceive your reality through. We ask you to listen deeper, deeper than any system that has become a part of your consciousness in your experience as a human being on the planet Earth.

And so let us begin together the sojourn from light, from the All, from the nothingness, to the moment in time, distance and form which you are experiencing as you hold this book.

Part of the game that you, collectively as humans have created is the game of overcoming pain, suffering and fear. These experiences on the planet have been part of the lessons that you chose to learn. These experiences are attached to the gameboard you chose to play on. These experiences are no longer necessary. Earth is crying. The Earth itself has had enough of these experiences and she wishes now to shift her polarity, to shift the axis, to shift away from the duality that lives in the realm of good and evil.

Do not fear. The shift in polarity will take place in consciousness or in physical manifestation. The shift itself is inevitable. The form the shift takes is up to you and your brothers and your sisters, the other sparks of light here, manifesting in physical form. There are those among you who have come to this planet, expressly to be a part of this shift. You have come here, (or been sent) to be available to participate in the shift of consciousness. Your sojourn on this planet began many, many millennia ago.

The plan for the planet Earth has been very carefully constructed. Your part in that plan is now dawning on your awareness. As you read these pages, those of you who are here to participate in the mission of shifting the consciousness of this planet are hearing, deep within yourselves a very, very familiar chord. This knowledge has been shut off to you in its fullness until this time. That also is part of the plan, part of the game that you, and we constructed in the beginning of time.

Each spark, as it left, as it separated, as it delineated itself from the whole, experienced its own isolation. And in that isolation, there was the experience of pain, for separateness and pain go hand in hand. When one experiences oneself as separate from the whole there is, in the isolation the experience of pain and the experience of suffering.

The illusion of pain and suffering is the illusion of separateness. In these pages, we hope, that you will discover your own personal experience of separateness, and hence of pain and suffering has been illusionary.

Being cut off from God is the source of all suffering. Human beings have cut themselves off from the experience of the God within them. It is time to open up your consciousness fully to experience the core of your own being. That core is God. No duality, no experience of evil is necessary for you to experience the truth of who you are. Who you are is a spark of God, a hologram, containing all, existing everywhere, reflecting everything. Who you are is consciousness, pure energy, light.

SEE foreward

We on the planet Venus and others of us in myriad other dimensions, both physical and non-physical, have been watching the development of the planet Earth and the development of the human mind. The experiment in duality has reached its full flower. The evidence of this is the threat of nuclear holocaust now present on the planet. This holocaust will take place if the shift away from the duality of good is not completed within this century.

It is not good or bad which way you, collectively on Earth, choose to manifest the shift. It is more expedient to choose the shift in consciousness rather than physical destruction. If physical destruction takes place, which is to say, if enough of the collective mind does not choose a shift in consciousness, a raising of consciousness toward God, toward good, toward pure energy, then the energy which man, in his clinging to duality, has synthesized and compressed within the bomb will be the expression of the choice for duality.

As the shift is made, vast areas of the planet may, indeed change their form as an expression of the shift. Cities along the coastline of the United States, cities on the coastline of Asia, may indeed, crumble. This, though apparently horrible, will be a manifestation of the cleansing of consciousness. Those of you who participate in the cleansing, in the lifting of consciousness, need not fear the physical shifting of the surface of the planet.

The degree of the shift is not yet determined. That is why the prophesies are not coordinated. The degree of the shift on the surface of the planet will reflect the degree of the shift away from duality, the degree of the shift toward the pole of God, toward the pole called God. If the choice of the consciousness on the planet is to cling to duality then the destruction will be final at last and Earth herself will split.

Duality is the experience of separateness. Duality is the source of pain. The isolation one experiences in the realm of duality is the pain of being separate from God. Evil is not necessary to experience God. Oneness, Isness is all that is necessary. This experience of Isness, or oneness is being promulgated by many disciplines and many groups now surfacing on the planet. These groups are part of what has been called the Aquarian Conspiracy. It is a conspiracy because it was planned eons ago when the game began. If you are a part of this conspiracy, if you are a part of the consciousness which chose the mission of coming to this planet to be present at this time and participate in the choice that is now facing the human mind, you will know it by the time you finish reading this book. We invite you to dis-cover yourself.

CHAPTER TWO

In that beginning you were one of the sparks separating from the Isness. In choosing to come to Earth and experience humanness, you also chose a human mind. The human mind contains the record of all experiences that you, as an individual spark have known. The human mind also contains access to all experiences every other spark has known, human and not human. All sparks existing in every dimension are linked into a universal mind. Through your individual mind you can connect with the universal mind. That is the way this book is being written. You have the power with-in you to connect with the universal mind at any time that you are willing to disconnect and rise above your individual mind. Your individual mind has a series of thought systems, a series of thought patterns, a series of connections. Frequently, these thought patterns, these systems and connections are referred to as karma.

In choosing to come to Earth, in choosing the human mind, you choose to experience the system associated with what has been called karma. Karma is part of the illusion connected to the illusion called Earth. The series of illusions you have chosen to experience are unique to you. The systems, patterns, connections that your mind has made and is making are yours alone. However, even though they are unique, there is a pattern to the pat-tern. Those patterns that you have adopted have shaped your point of view and your point of view has created your reality. Just as it is possible to rise above or transcend your individual mind and to connect with universal mind, it is also possible to transcend or rise above your own patterns, that is to say, to rise above your own karmic system. The system that you developed for your own particular karma, that is to say, your own particular sojourn on the planet Earth is one that you adopted for specific reasons, to match your own specific destiny. Destiny has been created by you, for you, out of those patterns which you choose to adopt.

When we, collectively, within the universal mind, designed and planned the game associated with Earth and humanness, we, collectively, foresaw the interplay of the system of duality referred to as good and evil. It has been an experiment. It has been a series of experiences designed by each of us and by all of us, to move toward the polarity farthest away from good. That movement is now at its outward swing and it is time to return.

It is now time to end the system of duality. That system has been so long associated with the human mind that there is much fear and resistance associated with abandoning that system.

Within each human mind is the thought that abandoning the system of duality, that is to say of no longer choosing to experience that which we call evil, will be followed by the destruction of the individual. The individual has so embedded himself in the system that he has lost his own experience of his own connection to the universal, to God and to truth.

The resistance to the abandoning of duality, the resistance to the abandoning of evil must be sloughed off. The resistance within yourself to your own clinging to evil, to your own clinging to those thought patterns that have produced, on the planet Earth, war, hunger, ecological problems, ecological destruction must be abandoned. You have the choice and the opportunity to rise above those systems, to rise above your individual mind in its clinging to the patterns of duality and to associate yourself with the original Isness within you, reflecting you, surrounding you, filling you.

When the planet Earth was called into existence, through our mutual creation, when the game of duality, of good and evil was designed as an experience for human beings to choose to participate in, in their sojourn on the planet Earth, we, collectively foresaw this time, this time when the swing in the polarity called evil would have reached its maximum breaking point. Within this century, that time has been reached. Those of you who have come to the planet to participate in the swing back toward the polarity of good are now being called through these pages to remember yourself, to remember your mission. The mission is part of the game as well. Part of the game you choose to play.

The outcome of the game does not have ultimate significance. What-ever the outcome is we will, collectively choose another form for the game. The mission is not significant. The mission is not a burden. The mission is an opportunity for you individually and collectively to choose within yourself to experience God. That choice is a joy. These pages provide a pathway into your own heart.

The ultimate destiny is God. Time and space are illusions, hence it is of no significance how long it takes to reach God since time ultimately doesn't exist. However, pain, suffering and fear have taken their toll on the human experience. The purpose of life, the purpose of experiencing joy and knowing oneself fully can no longer be participated in by imbuing oneself with pain and with suffering. Those things have been part of our mutual creation. They have been reflections of the potential of the Isness.

Every being who has ever manifested himself in physical form on the planet Earth has participated in the creation of the duality called evil. Every being on the planet Earth and those that will come in future generations, if such there be, has already reflected that part of himself referred to as evil. It is now time to begin fully reflecting the opposite pole, the pole referred to as good. There is an opportunity now on the planet Earth to move away from evil, to end suffering, to end pain, to end war, to restore the crying planet Earth to her own goodness.

The choice for goodness, the choice for God, joy and celebration is a choice that you, as an individual, have the opportunity to make. Since your individual mind is connected to universal mind, the choice you make makes an impact on all other human and non-human forms. That is why we ask you to look within your own heart and see what choice you will make.

Those of you who came to the planet from beyond eons ago have once stated that given this opportunity, your choice would be to bring joy, to eliminate suffering. That choice is presented to you now. Once again, you have the opportunity to make that choice. You have the opportunity to fulfill the commitments you once made. The choice has many facets. The choice witnesses itself in your daily life, in your thought, in your work, in your relationships. Each moment is an opportunity for you to rechoose. At the same time, having once made that choice, having chosen to come to the planet to be present at this time when the planet itself, when the universal consciousness associated with the planet Earth is, collectively making that choice, you have also chosen to participate in the major shift now approach-ing. The form of the contribution to that shift may vary greatly. It may even now be different than the one you originally perceived it to be. How-ever, your participation is imperative.

In the system referred to as karma, that is to say, the system associated with the individual human mind, within that system, certain decisions are made as one experiences the reality one has created. Those decisions then shape and delineate one's future experience of one's subsequent creation. In experiencing further creations, further realities, more decisions are made. Those decisions build on each other. Those decisions form patterns. Those decisions shape your point of view. Your point of view is that through which you, not only perceive your reality but through which you also create your reality.

In choosing to come to Earth, you choose to participate in this system. The system has been very useful. It has allowed you to experience many, many reflections of the Isness. Each choice that you have made to participate in a particular reality has allowed you to come to know that part of your self which that reality reflects. The choices you have made have been purely individual, however they have been associated with your individual human mind, that is to say, they have been associated with the illusion of separateness.

The human mind experiences itself as separate and isolated from others, locked into the system of duality. Duality as a system presupposes twoness, that is to say it presupposes separation. This separation also is existent in one's experience of God or goodness, that is to say, within the human system, God and goodness are experienced as separate from oneself. This is an illusion. This is not true. This is the fault of the system of duality. That system has served its purpose. That system has allowed you to experience reflections of the Isness, to experience myriads of realities which otherwise you would not have called into existence and therefore not known that part of yourself. Evil is not ultimately bad. Evil has been part of the Isness, reflecting the potential to experience and that part of the reflection of the Isness is now completing itself. There is an opportunity for that part of the system to fold in on itself and in folding in on itself to disappear. You are invited to participate in the game that holds the completion of evil.

You are a spark of light that chose to manifest yourself in physical form on the planet Earth. Others of us chose other game gameboards. Some of these gameboards exist in physical space and may be referred to as planets. Physical form manifests itself throughout this universe and other dimensional universes in a vast variety.

Those of you on Earth in choosing your humanness also chose a human mind. The human mind in the experience on Earth is linked to the system of karma. Participating in the system of karma presupposes decisions within the individual human mind based on past experiences. Since the human mind is associated with the planet Earth the decisions which you have made and from which you have created your own individual karmic pattern are limited to the experiences on this planet. You have had many, many, many other experiences in other dimensions both non-physical and physical. Many of you have had existences on other planets in forms resembling those that are called human. Many of you have had experiences in other forms. The forms are not import- ant. What is important is the consciousness or the level of awareness which inhabited each physical form.

![Fellowship For Today logo] *Learning · Living · Love TOGETHER*

Fellowship For Today
Spiritual Center

LIBRARY CHECKOUT CARD

You are preparing a permanent record for our library, so please print or write legibly.

Title
A Call to The Light workers

Author (Last, First)
Powers, Ehea

☑ Book ☐ CD/Tape ☐ DVD/Video

☐ Other (Please specify): _____ _____
Category

To check out this library book / item, remove this check out card from the library book / item then, on the back of this card, enter your name, phone number & check out date and place it in the Library check out box.

													Full Name - Phone
													Check Out Date

Many of the forms that you have inhabited in other spaces, and other dimensions would seem strange to you by your human judgement. However those forms may well have had a consciousness much more open, much more aware than that consciousness which you are now experiencing. Those forms that you have known on other planets in other dimensions continue to exist. Many of those forms have consciousnesses far more open to truth than the consciousness you are now experiencing in your human form. Those other consciousnesses, those consciousness associated with other forms, other planets, other dimensions of physical reality have been very much in tune with the experiment of duality existing on the planet Earth.

There has been much controversy on Earth about the existence of life on other planets. Life exists not only on other planets in this solar system, in this galaxy, in this dimensional universe, there are multi-millions of other dimensional universes co-existing with the one you are familiar with.

Other dimensional universes manifest themselves in a variety of form and in many degrees of physical and non-physical manifestations. There are many gradations between physical and non-physical. Consciousness is not only associated with form. In addition to other physical manifestations, other physical universes, there are also consciousnesses existing in non-physical dimensions. How could it be otherwise since all there is is ultimate Isness. Everything, therefore, holds within itself the consciousness of Is. That is to say, everything is a part of that which you have called God.

The consciousness of all dimensions of physical form, non-physical forms, the consciousness of the Isness has been aware of the experiment in duality taking place on Earth. The consciousness has been watching.

Many other physical forms, that is to say, the consciousness associ-ated with other physical forms in other dimensions, have been aware of the struggle within the system of duality existing on Earth. This consciousness has been watching. It has been watching, both in a very real physical sense from what you might call, space stations, hovering within this galaxy and also from non-physical conscious-ness, both within your atmosphere and without. The appearance of physical UFOs on the surface of the planet and associated with the surface of this planet is quite real. Their presence re-presents the concern and the support of the consciousness of the Isness in the Earth's struggle with duality.

It has been difficult for the human mind to conceive of life beyond its own form, of life or consciousness existing in other forms from other places. The consciousness of other universes, of other physical form, need not be feared. The experiment in duality is limited to life on Earth. That is to say, physical forms not associated with Earth do not participate in the experiment in good and evil. Therefore, your brothers and sisters in space bring no harm to the planet Earth. Evil does not exist within their consciousness. Many of them have chosen previous life experiences within the human system on this planet. They are therefore familiar with the duality within the human mind. Many of them came to experience humanness for a period on the planet so that they would be aware of the mechanisms within the system at play during the time of the shift. They have been preparing, as you have been preparing, for their participation in this next phase of the experience on Earth.

Your brothers and sisters from other dimensions and other universes and other planets within your system, as we are within your system, though not within your dimension, have come to assist you and support you in raising the vibration of the consciousness on Earth, so that the duality that holds the system of good and evil may be completed.

There are other systems of physical reality, other planets, other dimensions in which experiments similar to the experiments on Earth have been made. Those experiences, in other dimensions have completed them-selves. That is why we are aware of the mechanism in play at this time on Earth.

It is accurate that time is an illusion. Time is associated with distance, space and form. Therefore, in the illusion of distance, space and form, time is necessary. Therefore, these other planets, existing in form and space have also existed within the system, though illusionary, of time. It is therefore possible for us to say that the experiments, similar to the one on Earth, have already completed themselves. Within the illusion, they are in the past. However, within that illusion, many of you, having participated in those experiments, carry memories of destruction.

The destruction that has taken place on other planets, in other systems in other experiments of the Isness need not take place on the planet Earth. You know this. You chose to come to this planet to experience the completion of your own duality.

We, in other dimensions — physical and non-physical, lend you our support, lend you our love, as you complete within yourselves your own experience of evil.

Those of you existing on Earth, existing in the system of karma, have chosen a pattern of creating your reality based on decisions you have made while associated with the human mind, so that those of you who bear within you the memory of destruction on other systems, in other dimensions, carry no decisions based on that destruction. However, you do carry, deep within you, the memory of times past. That memory has also contributed to the resistance you experience in playing your part in the lifting of the consciousness of Earth.

Having chosen to manifest yourself on this planet, in human form, within the Earth's system of mind, you have made many, many, many decisions. Those decisions are limited to your experience on this planet. However, the memory of the destruction has contributed to your resistance. It is difficult for you to begin again. There is the experience of failure associated with the destruction of other systems. Know that there has been no failure. All has been part of the plan that you and we created in the beginning.

That plan includes your participation. Those of you who have participated in a game similar to the one now drawing to a close on this planet, need not fear failure. The experience of failure is an interpretation. Failure exists only in the mind that labels it failure. Every system that has completed itself, in every dimension, physical and non-physical has been part of the perfect plan of the Isness, part of the plan we designed together in the beginning.

Those systems that have folded in upon themselves have contributed to your experience of the potential of the multi-faceted reflections of the Isness. It is time to begin again. It is time to begin anew. The completion of the system of duality associated with the planet Earth is necessary. It is time for that completion to be made. Your participation in that completion is essential.

CHAPTER THREE

Karma, being limited to Earth, carries within itself as a system, decisions that you as an individual have made in your sojourn on this planet. When you first arrived here the vibratory level that you experienced was a shock to your system. Manifesting yourself in physical form was an experience that varied greatly for each of you. Those of you who came from a dimension of solid physical form did not have as difficult a time in the transition. However, there are those among you who came from a less physical and, indeed, from non-physical forms of energy. For many of you, manifesting yourself in the slower, lower vibration associated with physical form on Earth was very difficult. In that difficulty, your decisions began. Those decisions are still locked within you. Those decisions have affected your participation in the mission you chose to play.

The decisions locked within your individual mind began the moment you manifested yourself on Earth. Many of you decided that the job on Earth was too difficult, was too hard for you to make happen. Having come from a plane of consciousness in which manifesting thought was much less difficult, you, some of you, decided that you did not have the ability, the capability, the potential to manifest your thought on this planet. This is false. You manifest your thought constantly. Every thought has energy. That energy is the energy of creation. It is through thought that all is created. Each thought that you have manifests itself in a reality.

Those thoughts that you link to the human mind in the system of duality have created that lean toward the pole of evil, have, in fact, created the distress, the discomfort and the despair associated with the system on Earth. Those thoughts are now being cleansed from your mind by your activities to open your awareness. Reading this book is part of those activities. As you look into your life you will see the other activities that you, particularly, recently, have been participating in. We commend you for your choice. We commend you for the choice that you made eons and eons ago to participate in this particular phase of the experience on Earth.

Choosing the polarity of good or God, within the core of your being is not an easy thing. Choosing that core has repercussions in all of your thoughts. That impact, those repercussions, include an impact on the universal mind. Each time you, personally, as an individual, choose to abandon the evil within your own thought you drop a bit of evil out of the collective mind. Each time in your daily life that you are given the opportunity to choose good, to let go of the clinging to separateness, to experience yourself as one with another, as one with the Earth, with nature, with all consciousness, each time you make that choice you have an impact on the universal mind. Thoughts do not come unbidden. Thoughts are created. You create your own thoughts. You have the power and the ability to create thoughts that represent the pole of God.

As you experience your thoughts you can let go of those thoughts that represent the pole of pain and suffering. You can choose, moment by moment, in your daily life to see the unity, to express the oneness of all that is. You are a part of the energy of the universe. You have mistakenly identified yourself as separate, as ego. Ego is associated with the system of the human mind. Ego is false. Separateness is false. At the same time it is the ego within you that you must destroy. This ego must be destroyed in the process of abandoning evil, in the process of abandoning separateness. The ego was designed to be destroyed. It is nothing to be feared. Ego itself is completing itself in a very natural, predicted manner.

You are not murdering ego. You are allowing it to complete itself. Each time that you choose to let go, even a little of the illusion of separateness, each time that you choose to see yourself in another, you are raising the consciousness of the planet Earth. Each time you see yourself as part of all that is, that oneness becomes more real, becomes more evident, is manifested within the experience of all human beings. Each thought you have makes an impact on the whole. There is no burden in this. This is part of the game you chose to play.

Ego is a manifestation of the human mind, existing within the human system on the planet Earth. Your own ego is part of the clinging to duality. Your ego sees you as separate from God. Your ego detaches you from your own experience of oneness. It is your ego that keeps you as less than you are. You are perfect Isness. You are all that there is, expressing itself in your unique human way. People think that it is the ego that gives one grandiose ideas about oneself. It is actually the opposite. It is the ego that limits you to thinking that you are the one inside your bag of bones.

Existing within your own particular human form is that part of the Isness which you chose to reflect. Your ego has identified itself as that part. Your ego, therefore, is committed to the persistence of separateness. It sees itself as a part of the whole. It experiences itself as delineated, as separate from others, from other parts of the whole. Your ego cannot recognize itself as God. Your ego can only recognize itself as separate from God. The ego is not evil. The ego is only limiting. By clinging to your own ego, you are clinging to your own separateness. That separateness has kept you away from the experience of God within you.

Ego death is a part of many religious patterns and disciplines of the planet Earth. The ego must die to itself. That is to say, the ego must be transcended for you, reading this book, to experience yourself as part of the oneness, as unified with the all. This is a threat to the ego. The ego resists getting itself and knowing itself as God. The ego has served a function in the system of duality. The ego has allowed the illusion of separateness to persist so that one could experience oneself as separate within the system of duality, within the system of good and evil. That system is now drawing to a close, and the ego is no longer needed. Your ego is part of you. Your ego can be transcended. Your ego can be included in your experience of all that is possible in experiencing yourself. The ego need not be a limit. The ego need not be an enemy. The ego can be included, can be held in your hand, can be transcended.

Transcending your own individual ego is part of your mission on Earth if you are to be a part of the completion of the system of duality. We will guide you in transcending that ego which you have so long identified as yourself. Who you are is so far, far beyond ego that your ego is merely a breath of wind in your face — it may make you blink your eyes for a moment, losing your connection to your true reality, but the moment is very brief in your whole experience.

The ego, in clinging to duality, has allowed us all to play the game of duality, to play the game of separateness. We are indebted to the ego, which we also created as part of the game. Ego need not be killed. To die to one's ego is not to cease as an individual. To die to one's ego is to transcend, is to transform your experience of who you are.

You created your own ego to experience separateness when you chose a human mind and human form on this Earth. Your ego, like your body, your emotions, your thoughts, is part of the human experience which you are responsible for.

The ego, linked to the human mind, existing within the system of duality needs to be transcended and befriended. It is your ally on the pathway of your experience. Befriend it. Do not allow it to limit your experience of who you are. It is your ego's job to keep you small, to keep you separate from your connection to all that is. That ego, while once appropriate, now needs to be transcended. On your journey back to your own experience of your connection to all that is, the ego is, like a pebble in your shoe — an annoyance, something to be removed, but not something to be hated.

To allow the ego within you to die, to transcend that ego, to allow it to fold in on itself, is to discover your true identity. When you identify with yourself as separate from other, as separate from your brothers and sisters, as different, that is the ego. When you identify yourself as better than your brothers and sisters, that is the ego. When you identify yourself as less than your brothers and sisters, that is the ego. As you identify yourself as separate in any way, as better, as worse, as above, as beneath, as wiser, as less wise, as more attractive, as less attractive, in any way that you choose to delineate yourself and separate yourself from your brothers and sisters, that is ego.

It is accurate that some of you manifest different parts of the Isness than others. Some of you manifest musical talent. Some of you manifest physical beauty. Some of you manifest facility with words. Some of you manifest physical movement in dance. Each of these is a joyous expression of that part of you which you cannot see in any other way. Each of these apparent differences are to be rejoiced in, are to be enjoyed, are part of the celebration of the Allness of the Isness that you are. These differences should be seen, not as separations, but as part of the celebration of yourself.

Ego, within the human system, is your link to those decisions that make up the pattern of your individual karma. Karma is linked to the ego because the experience of ego continues from lifetime to lifetime within your individual subconscious mind. Karma can be transcended because the ego can be transcended. Ego limits your experience to separateness. Ego defines you as different than your brothers and your sisters.

Karma is a system existing within duality. Karma is tied to the concept of good and evil, right and wrong, reward and punishment. The human mind, based on its individual ego, makes decisions which define itself as separate from other expressions of the Isness rather than as reflecting parts of the Isness that are also reflecting to it.

Parts of the Isness that have taken other forms of manifestation, other means of expressing themselves than you have, are ultimately not different from you. They are ultimately also you. Therefore, in an ultimate sense, you cannot do injury to yourself. That is to say, you cannot harm yourself, because it is you who are doing both the action and the receiving of the action. It is all you. You can only play a game within the system of human reality. However, in the system of duality the appearance of separateness calls forth the appearance of good and evil.

Since there is a part of you, deep within your core that knows, absolutely, the truth of who you are, knows that your ultimate essence is pure energy, is light, is God, is goodness, each time that there is an action, in the human game that appears to be created out of separation from the experience of your own essence, a decision is made. A decision is made about your worth, about your own goodness, or lack of it, a decision is made which further defines and separates you from your brothers and your sisters. Those decisions, as has been stated, pile up on each other, expand off of each other, and form a pattern called karma.

Within your own, individual unique karmic system, these decisions have shaped your consciousness and have shaped your reality, since your reality is, ultimately, created out of your consciousness. By consciousness, we refer to the conscious, alert human mind, existing in what you call, "every day reality". We are not referring, in this case, to the ultimate consciousness. The conscious mind has been divided, in the discipline of psychology, into the divisions of conscious, subconscious and super-conscious. We are, in this case, talking about the psychological conscious mind. The ego exists within the subconscious mind, if one were to use that discipline to define these distinctions. Karmic patterns exist within what is called the subconscious mind.

Much has been discussed in contemporary psychology and contemporary metaphysical disciplines about the dream state. The dream state is a connection to the subconscious mind. In the dream state one is able to complete karmic patterns. That is to say one can create the reality in a dream rather than create that reality in every day life. One can use a dream to complete a karmic pattern. Dreams are very useful. In this book we will be training you to use the dream state to complete karmic patterns so that you need no longer create physical manifestations of these patterns to pay yourself back for your participation in the system of duality called good and evil.

Your individual karmic pattern, linked to your individual human experiences associated with the planet Earth can be transcended. Your individual human mind can be re- linked to the universal mind. In linking to the universal mind you can rise above the system of karma. The system of karma is tied to the experiment in duality, the experience of good and evil associated with this planet. It is imperative that you begin rising above your own karmic patterns. As long as you, as an individual human mind exist and cling to the system of karma, you will continue to create evil within yourself and between your brothers and sisters and manifest it as a reality on the surface of the planet Earth. It is possible to transcend karma. It is possible to complete karma in non-physical realities so that duality need not continue to be created.

The human mind is so connected to the system of duality that it fears transcending its own karma. It fears that it is doomed to act out, to demonstrate its own punishment for its own supposed evil. It is not punishment that is being left behind. It is the system which contains the notion that punishment and evil have any reality.

When one imagines that one has done an action that is evil. that is a denial of the goodness within one, one imagines that one must be punished to demonstrate one's allegiance to goodness or God. Punishment is error. The error exists within the system of duality. Punishment promulgates evil. It does not diminish it. Punishing oneself is the same as punishing another.

The system of duality spirals outward. Evil begets evil. It is time for that system to spiral inward, to fold in on itself, to complete itself and disappear from the human experience. That system can disappear and the human experience can continue in love, and in light, and in joy as it does, this moment, in many other dimensions, on many other planets, in many other forms of existence.

We, on the planet Venus exist in a dimension where love, joy, light and celebration of our oneness is the only experience. The system of duality on Earth can, with your participation, fold in on itself, leaving nothing but goodness, joy and celebration in your hearts.

CHAPTER FOUR

In the dream state, you leave your attachment to your individual mind behind and connect with the universal mind. In the dream state it is possible to rise above ego, karma, and individual mind.

The dream state is useful for many things. It is a trap door, an escape, from the individual mind. The dream state can be used to astral travel, that is to say, to leave your attachment to your own individual human body behind and experience the flow of the Isness.

The individual human mind is attached to the individual body. When one does, or experiences, what is called astral projection, one leaves the attachment to the human body, the individual body, behind. One surrenders to the Isness. One experiences oneself beyond the limits of attachment to your individual human form.

The techniques for astral projection in the dream state have been discussed in several published books on the subject. However, we wish to include in these pages some instructions on the technique called astral projection. The benefit of astral projection is that it allows you to detach from identifying solely with your body. It allows you to experience yourself, and know yourself beyond that attachment.

The main recommendation for the experience of astral projection is that you feel safe in your location. That is to say, you know that you will not be interrupted either by noise or intrusion. If one is to connect with the universal through this technique it is wise to protect the body from any sudden jarring. Hence, a quiet, safe place is recommended. All one needs to do is lie on your back, hands at your side in an open posture, and then begin deep breathing, calling on your own guides, teachers and higher consciousness, which is to say, your own connection to God, to come and guide you in the experience.

Decide on a place you'd want to go: a friend, a favorite spot of beauty, and then as you are lying there, breathing deeply, ask your higher consciousness to guide you in the journey to the specified place. And then as you are breathing deeply, allow yourself to relax and imagine your own etheric body, the body you really inhabit, that body that is not tied to gravity, that body that is light, imagine that body gradually detaching itself from the walls and downward pull of your physical body. Imagine it rising slowly up and floating just an inch above your own body, and then continue to breathe deeply.

As you become detached, notice how safe it is. And then under the guidance of your own higher consciousness, think of your friend or the place of beauty you have previously selected and just keep thinking about that place until you experience being there. And then, when you have been there notice some detail that will give you clarity in the fact that you are actually present. And then return. Feel yourself hovering just above your body again and gradually sinking down into the body, becoming attached once again, in touch with the system of gravity and breathing deeply, relax back into your body, being there.

When you do this ask that one of your own spiritual quides or your Higher Consciousness to direct the experience so that, should you run into any illusions that are disquieting, they and not you, will deal with them. That is a good way to begin.

We recommend that you keep a pad of paper next to your bed, a dream journal to use in beginning to familiarize yourself with the uses of the dream state. If you are conscious enough of the process, that is to say, have not fallen asleep, when you return and are securely back in your body, roll over and pick up your pad of paper and pen and write down your experience. It is good to acknowledge your Higher Consciousness and your guides for being your partner in the experience.

It is also possible, as previously stated, to use the dream state for the completion of karmic patterns. The purpose in using the dream state as a tool in this matter, is to allow you to complete those patterns associated with the system of karma in the reality known as the dream state rather than in the reality of your daily life.

Many people use their dreams in this fashion. Few people, however, are conscious of the fact that they are doing this. As you become more conscious and aware of using your dreams in this manner, you will be able to complete karmic patterns in the dream state rather than in your daily life. You will be able to do this volitionally.

For example: if you notice, in your daily life, a particular pattern, a particular animosity, a particular limitation, that you sense you are placing on yourself, make a note of it during the day. It may be that there is a particular person that you experience rivalry, competition, animosity with.

In the beginning of your human sojourn you made various decisions that have kept you locked within the patterns of karma. Those patterns must be transcended for you to regain your experience of your true identity. Those patterns, rather than being manifested in your personal, physical reality, can be completed, can be transcended by using the dream state. In the dream state you have contact with your subconscious mind. The subconscious mind is the storehouse of all of your individual karmic patterns. It is expedient and appropriate to use the dream state to complete these patterns.

The technique is easy. We recommend that you begin keeping a journal, or a pad of paper and pen at your bedside. Begin training yourself to write down those patterns you wish to transcend or to break out of just before you go to sleep. Write the pattern on the pad of paper, then, as you drift off to sleep, be recalling the pattern and asking your guides, your spiritual allies, to assist you in the realm of your subconscious mind to break those patterns in the dream state. You may do that as follows: perhaps in the daily life, for example, you have noticed that you have a fear associated with being part of a large group of people. As you go to sleep, write on your tablet that you wish, or intend to break out of the pattern of fear associated with large groups of people. Then, as you drift off to sleep, hold in your mind the thought that this evening, this night, this period of sleeping you will transcend that pattern. Then trust. Allow those spiritual helpers who are with you always, but more accessible to you in your dream state to assist you.

It is not necessary that you recall the dream. The dream will complete the pattern whether you recall it or not. Begin to train yourself to write down those parts of the dream that you recalled when you first awakened. This method of writing down the dream when you awaken will allow your conscious mind to begin to develop more control of the dream state. If you do not at first recall the dream, do not be concerned. Continue the discipline. Those parts of the dream that you do recall, may not, in the beginning, seem to be related to the pattern you chose to transcend the evening before. However, the fabric of the subconscious mind is closely woven and each thread is a part of that pattern. Each time one thread is broken the fabric weakens. Do not attempt to understand how the fabric is put together. Just trust.

In your waking hours you may begin to notice your reactions to a particular pattern. You may begin to notice a shift in the way you interact in your day to day experience with that particular pattern. In the example given you may notice that the next time you are in a large group of people your customary thought pattern has shifted, even if only in a small degree. Continue to work on a particular pattern until the shift has reached the desired point of transformation. That is to say, you may notice that you are slightly less fearful in a group situation. You may begin to have insights into your participation, through your thought patterns, in creating the fear you experience in a particular circumstance.

Allow your conscious mind to notice each shift. Some of the shifts may be small, may be imperceptible to your awareness, however, whether or not your conscious mind is aware of the process, the system works. Play with it. Continue to concentrate on a particular pattern until the fabric of that pattern has been completely unraveled. There will come a time, if you continue, to focus on the example given, for instance, when the fear that you once experienced in association with large groups of people has shifted to the point where you notice its absence.

What you will be doing by using this technique is transcending your own karmic pattern of decisions that you have made in each reality you have created. Eventually there will no longer be the need, because the decisions have been transcended, to create realities in which these patterns are manifested. You will be freeing yourself from your own karmic system.

In freeing yourself from this system, you will be transcending your own individual human mind. You will be allowing yourself to transcend the thoughts connected with your own experience of separateness. You will be allowing yourself to gradually, once again experience yourself as part of all that is. The karmic system of decisions and patterns in your individual subconscious mind are, in part, responsible for your experience of your own separateness. Karma can be completed in the dream state using this technique.

As we have suggested, then, the dream state is a useful tool for your conscious mind to use in transcending your attachment to your physical form, and therefore to the illusion of physical separateness. Through the developed experience of detaching yourself from the physical form in the dream state you can experience yourself in that state of transcendence as part of the larger All. The dream state can also be used to transcend karma.

We invite you to play with your dreams so that in the end, all of your dreams may come true.

CHAPTER FIVE

The illusion of separateness, the illusion of ego, the illusion of individual mind can also be transcended in the state of meditation. Many, many disciplines on Earth have used this technique to transcend the individual mind and experience one's connection with All That Is. This technique is useful. This technique, however, is more or less useful according to individual states of awareness and individual karmic decisions.

Some of you who have attempted to transcend the individual mind through the use of this technique, have experienced obstacles. Those obstacles are related to your own karmic patterns. For example, it is possible that in a previous life experience associated with your human sojourn, you experienced a lifetime in which meditation was a principle discipline. It could be that you made decisions associated with the use of that technique. It could be that the experience of that lifetime or of an event in that lifetime, was excruciatingly uncomfortable. Therefore, in that lifetime the decisions connected with that activity, are blocking your experience of success in using that technique. In this case, it will first be necessary for you to use another technique, another system to transcend the barriers to your own successful use of the technique of meditation.

Meditation is ultimately very, very useful. That is why it has been used for so long by so many masters. In mastering the technique of meditation, one masters the transcendence of separateness.

Those of you who have had difficulty in mastering meditation need first to remove your individual, karmicly associated obstacles to the use of this technique. Therefore we recommend the use of the dream state, or other techniques later to be mentioned, to transcend your own obstacles on the pathway to mastering the use of meditation as a technique in transcending your individual mind.

Many systems on Earth, many religions, many disciplines have promulgated various techniques for mastering the use of meditation. It may be that one of these techniques, the use of a mantra for instance, or the use of focusing on a flame, the use of focusing on a particular master, the use of focusing on a particular sound, the use of focusing on your breathe, the use of focusing on a particular location associated with a chakara in your body, may be useful to you. It is possible that the obstacle that you experience in association with one technique, you do not associate with another. However, the basic act of meditation has many parallels regardless of the technique applied. These parallels are enough to trigger your own karmic decisions associated with the process of meditation. It may even be, for example: that in an ancient life experience you were simply sitting on a mountain top, peacefully observing the view, when your body was attacked by a mountain lion. It could be that that attack led to your death.

In the human mind the decision that sitting peacefully in contemplation leads to death could be responsible, for example, to your resistance to the process of meditation. If you use the dream state to remove, transcend, or break the pattern of resistance associated with the process of meditation, your dreams will soon unravel those decisions associated with whatever event in your individual karmic system is blocking you in your experience of mastery of the technique of meditation. In other words, you may use one technique to master the use of another technique designed to eliminate, designed to transcend your experience of separateness.

Meditation is one technique that you can use to transcend your individual mind. In meditation you can link up with the universal mind. By linking up with the universal mind you, in transcending your individual separateness, can experience your personal connection to all that is. That is to say, by allowing yourself to identify yourself with the flow of consciousness beyond your own unique thought system, you are experiencing a truer reality than the one you are personally attached to and personally creating in your everyday life.

Many systems of meditation advanced by many disciplines on Earth focus on the breath. The breath is a constant connection with consciousness beyond the limits of your own physical form. Air itself has consciousness. Each time you breathe you are pulling in to your own body, consciousness. This consciousness that you call air is part of the connection that you share with all other living forms on Earth. The air itself is a link between you and others. The air itself belies your own experience of separateness, since each time you breathe you are pulling in consciousness that connects you to all other living forms on Earth.

In many parts of the Earth's atmosphere that consciousness itself is being polluted. This pollution is a sadness beyond the much discussed ecological problems created by the destruction of clarity in the air. This pollution represents clouded consciousness. It is a manifestation in physical form of the clouded consciousness that exists on the planet. The consciousness on Earth has become clouded, has become polluted with impurities manufactured by man. Manufactured by the human mind in his loss of identification with All That Is.

The clouded consciousness represented by the pollution of the air is the product of man's loss of partnership, loss of respect, for the nature that surrounds him. This nature does not only consist of trees, streams, other forms of life, plant and animal. Nature herself is consciousness. The separation from nature out of which man has created mechanisms that cloud or pollute the air or consciousness is a representation of the loss of connection with nature, with consciousness, with clarity, purity and truth.

The cloud of pollution hovering above many cities on Earth is a manifestation of the pollution of man's own consciousness and the separation he experiences from his own nature. It is there as a warning. It is there as a symbol. As man begins to wake up to the clouding of his own consciousness and take measures to eliminate the pollution of the air, the clouds of impurity will be lifted from the physical air and from his own consciousness. Man will again, if he chooses to purify the air and eliminate the constant pollution of it, experience clarity in his own consciousness. Each time man breathes in polluted air he is contributing to the symbolic pollution of his own awareness.

Man has polluted this awareness with the system of good and evil existing on Earth. The pollution of the air hovering above cities is a physical manifestation of the pollution of consciousness inherent in the system of duality. Each time you see yourself as separate than that which surrounds you, as not caring what effect your own mechanisms have on that which surrounds you, you contribute to the pollution of consciousness. Each time you put your own comfort and ease above the welfare of that which surrounds you, you separate yourself from the truth of who you are. Your own individual experience of joy and celebration, would not, in the natural course of events, contribute to the dis-ease of those people and things in your environment. Your environment is truly as much a part of who you are as your own physical body is.

Systems of meditation based on the breath were designed to connect you consciously with your connection to the consciousness that links you to your brothers and sisters. By focusing on your breath in meditation, you are focusing on that link which denies separateness. The air is the link to the consciousness that each of you participate in. As you breathe that consciousness into your body and focus your awareness on the fact that you are doing that, you are focusing your awareness on the link that joins you to all other animate, breathing manifestations of the Isness.

The technique of concentrating on your breath as you sit quietly in a location where intrusion is prevented, where disturbances are minimized, and focus on your breath, focus on drawing into yourself that consciousness that links you to all others on the surface of the planet, you are transcending separateness. The apparent physical isolation may seem to contribute to your own idea that you are a separate individual. However, if in the physical isolation, you concentrate on drawing into yourself the consciousness you share with your brothers and sisters, you can use this technique to begin to transcend your own isolation.

As you pull the breath in, sitting in a comfortable position, focus on the unity that connects you with all life. As you exhale focus on your own individual connection to that unity, your own individual contribution to the consciousness that unites you with your brothers and your sisters on Earth. Drawing the breath in represents the connection of the universal to you the individual. Exhaling represents your individual connection to the universal. The universal contributes to you, you contribute to the universal. You are connected to all that is. You are connected to all life.

You, in your physical manifestation, are dependent upon the air you breathe. This also may be seen symbolically. Your individual experience is fully dependent upon the universal consciousness. That is to say, without your connection to the universal consciousness, represented by the air that you breathe into your individual form, your individual experience could not persist. Equally true, if you did not exhale, if you did not contribute out of yourself into the universal consciousness, your individual form could not exist. Your continual connection, the flow in and out from the universal to you and from you to the universal is necessary to sustain life. As you meditate and focus on the breath, use this symbolic representation to experience your own unique connection to the universal.

The symbolism of the breath may also be used in a more sociological or psychological distinction. That is to say, as you allow the universal, represented in physical form by your brothers and sisters to contribute to you, as you accept and receive into yourself the flow from others, your own aliveness is sustained. Likewise, it is impossible to withhold your own contribution to others and maintain your own aliveness. This give and take between you and those around you and those even beyond your knowing, is necessary to sustain life in a physiological, psychological, philosophical and spiritual delineation. Therefore, as you allow your brothers and sisters to contribute to you, your aliveness is enhanced. As you pull up from yourself, your own resources and contribute them to those around you, your own aliveness is sustained and enhanced.

The give and take between life forms is necessary for life to continue. Therefore, allow those around you to contribute to you, to share their gifts, their resources, their essence with you. You do not need to deserve it. It is the way it is. Deserving has nothing to do with it. The function of give and take between human beings, and indeed, those of you with pets may want to include other living forms, is a necessary function of life. Worthiness is not a factor.

Feelings of unworthiness and undeservedness stem from decisions in the karmic pattern. Karma is linked to duality and separateness. Feelings of unworthiness, feelings that you do not deserve to receive or to have, or to express, are all based on karmic decisions within the system of good and evil. If one thinks one did something evil, one thinks one doesn't deserve. One thinks one needs to be punished by either withholding oneself, out of feeling unworthy to contribute to the flow of life, or by refusing to allow in that flow of gifts from others. This is all contradictory to the basic flow of life. It is all rooted in karmic patterns associated with duality. You deserve to receive in the same way that you deserve to breathe in air. You deserve to express in the same way that you deserve to exhale. You would not question your deserving to breathe, likewise you should not question your deserving to receive from the flow of life represented frequently by your brothers and sisters, nor your deserving to express yourself, to contribute your gifts to the flow of life also frequently represented by your brothers and sisters. The give-and-take between you and others is as necessary as your own breathing to sustain your life and the life of those around you.

As you practice meditation, focusing on your breath, focus on the flow of life into your body. Focus on the flow of life into your experience. Focus on the flow of life out of your body. Focus on your contribution to all that is.

CHAPTER SIX

In the beginning of your sojourn on the planet Earth you made many decisions. These decisions are part of the karmic pattern you have woven through your experiences in the human form. These patterns have brought your experience forward, lifetime, after lifetime, after lifetime. These pat-terns have molded your thought patterns. These patterns have filtered and created your experience. These patterns are present in your mental system as you read this book. These thought patterns can be transcended. These patterns can be broken.

There are many methods available to you to transcend these patterns. We have discussed the use of dreams. We have discussed the use of meditation. We will now discuss the use of dream analysis to disclose and hence transcend, by choice, these patterns. It is useful to keep a journal of your dreams. In addition to using the dream state to willfully train yourself to break patterns in your sleeping hours, you may also use the dreams, created by your subconscious mind to discover, explore and break those patterns which generate your reality.

The dream state is as useful as the waking state. In some cases, the dream state can be more useful than the waking state to discover your own patterns. For example: if you frequently experience dreams in which you are fleeing, or running away from some apparent threat, you may notice that you have a pattern in your subconscious mind that represents and creates the thought of being threatened by an outside force. This pattern, though perhaps apparent to you only in the dream state through the symbolic representation of the dreams created by your subconscious mind is also present in your awakened state, though perhaps less defined and identifiable.

If you have repeated dreams, to use this example, of being pursued by someone or something it is perhaps rooted in the thought, as a subconscious level, that there is a threat to you from without. It is obvious that the thought that there is an external threat is rooted in duality, in a system of them or me. The thought of an external threat cannot, obviously, come from a thought grounded in oneness. The idea of separateness is the basis of all fear. Fear is the apparency of separateness and, hence, of injury, personal harm or destruction at some level of what you consider yourself. The threat may be perceived as injury to your physical well being or to your emotional or psychological well being. It is apparent that the thought of a threat of outside injury of any kind cannot come from the realization of your unity with all things.

The threat of outside injury is rooted in duality. Fear is rooted in duality. Fear presupposes separateness. Fear is tied to the illusion of the thought that you are separate from your brothers and your sisters in consciousness. If you truly experience your unity with all that is, your oneness with the all, your connection to all consciousness, you would not experience fear. You would know that no harm can come to you from yourself.

Fear belongs to the system of good and evil. Fear imagines evil and perceives evil in any manifestation, at any level, as a threat to oneself. It is obvious that the thought of injury from without presupposes that one is victim to one's reality. It obviously cannot come from the true realization that one is the creator of one's experience of one's reality. Fear is an illusionary emotion because it is based on the illusion of good and evil. Each time you, as an individual, experience fear of any kind, on any level, you are participating in the illusion of duality.

When you experience a fearful dream you have the opportunity to discover one of your patterns that ties you to the illusion of duality. The use of a journal to write down your dreams at the moment of waking, is an opportunity for you to discover those patterns that separate you from the experience of your own divinity. As the creator of all that exists in your personal reality, you are in charge of the game. There is no external force, or external consciousness that can intrude or threaten your own creation. You create it all. If you are creating fear as a part of your experience, you are creating illusions in the system of duality.

It is useful to begin to train yourself to use the dream state by keeping a pad of paper and a pen by the side of your sleeping area and writing down before you go to sleep, those patterns, one at a time (work on one pattern until the result is produced in your waking hours) just before you drift off to sleep. Hold in mind as you sleep, the thought that you will use the night's sleeping hours to begin to unravel the pattern. Then, when you wake in the morning immediately write down any dream, any experience that you recall from the hours of sleep. Hence, you will be using the journal before you go to bed and as you first wake up.

It will take some discipline to recall your dreams. You need not write down every detail of the dream. Just recall the dream and ask yourself what pattern in the system of duality this dream holds. Then on a page in your journal begin to make a list of those patterns that you recognize. In the example given the pattern represents the fear of injury from without. Another dream may hold a basic story line of aggression, that is to say, of injury imposed on an external consciousness from within your personal consciousness. Once again, this feeling is rooted in the system of duality, of separateness. Make a list of those patterns which you recognize as part of the system of duality.

It is useful to also begin to note those dreams which are joyous, which represent a celebration of unity and connection to other consciousnesses. As you record and recall the experiences of oneness and joy in the dream state you will be underscoring that experience, you will be telling your subconscious mind that you are willing and able to experience unity and joy. You will be developing your capacity for increased creation of celebration. In impressing upon yourself this ability to create and experience joy and celebration you will be deepening your connection to the wonder available in the human experience.

It is useful therefore, to recall and record all of your dreams, whether they represent a pleasant or an unpleasant experience. The unpleasant experiences are part of the pattern that hold you in the system of duality. The pleasant experiences reveal your capacity to create joy. As you begin breaking patterns in the dream state that connect you to the system of duality, you will be creating experiences in the dream state that reveal your ability to create purely positive reality. You will begin to see that you have the power to create realities for yourself to experience which can be either positive or negative. You will be developing your inner knowledge that you are in charge of creating your reality. For who but you creates your dreams?

The dream state, as has been stated, can thus be used to transcend your attachment to physical separateness, to break karmic patterns, and reveal to yourself your own ability to create reality. There may be other interesting things that you notice in your dreams. You may notice your connection to particular people, to particular locations or particular activities. These connections can also reveal to you inner sources of creative expression. Your dream is a creative expression of your subconscious mind. Pleasant, joy-filled dreams reveal to you your ability to create joy in yourself and, hence, in your brothers and your sisters. Each of us has the potential to create vast amounts of joy through many forms of expression on Earth.

If for example, in the dream state, you find yourself creating a joyous expression through the use of dance, you may wish, in your waking hours to study dance, or to further develop your ability in that area. If, in your dream state, you discover your ability to produce the experience of joy through communication, verbal, written or through artistic expression, you may wish, during your waking hours, to focus on developing that ability of expression. As you begin to focus on your own ability for positive creation you will begin to focus your conscious mind on the pole associated with goodness and God. As you begin to fill your waking state with constructive thoughts of positive expression you begin to anchor your conscious mind in the polarity called good.

Positive activity develops your capacity for positive experience. Hence, studying or practicing dance, for example, as opposed to filling your time with an activity less joyous, perhaps even brooding over problems, develops your connection to the experience of joy and weakens your connection to the experience of less than joyous emotions and thoughts. Therefore, we recommend that you notice negative experiences in your dreams and list them as patterns to be transcended and that you also record positive experiences in your dreams as experiences to be consciously developed in your awakened state.

Some nights you may astral travel. Some nights you may, in a deep somnambulant level — perhaps not even remembered in the morning, be breaking karmic patterns. You may also dream. In truth most of you do all three of these activities in your sleep. Sometimes the sleeping hours are devoted to only one or two, in various combinations, of these possible experiences in the dream state. As you use your journal you will be developing your awareness of yourself beyond which you normally experience in the conscious, waking state. You will see that your consciousness transcends your own daily conscious thought patterns. You will begin to experience more of the truth of who you really are.

You, as a spark of light, existing, or manifesting yourself as a human on Earth at this time in the history of the planet, have chosen to participate in the shift of polarity rapidly approaching the Earth. The form of that participation is up to you. You may be one who resists the shift, or you may be one who does not. You may be one who participates in guiding, or leading, or facilitating, or demonstrating, by your example, others. Each of you has the opportunity in this lifetime to complete your own experience of duality. Each of you remembering your mission as you read this book, has the opportunity to assist others in completing their participation in the experiment of good and evil.

The form of your participation is ultimately not important. All that is ultimately important for you to keep your promise, for you to fulfill your mission, is the willingness to begin. You will find your own form. However, many of you have an affinity for a particular form of expression. Some of you express your Isness, your connection to all that is, and indeed experience it through dance. Some of you experience and express your divinity through music. Some of you express who you truly are by running a corporation or a business with integrity. Some of you, and this includes all children under ten, express who you are by just being yourself and sharing yourself with those around you.

You can use your dreams to discover, if you haven't already, what form of expression is most appropriate for you. The trick, however, is to begin. Many of you have already begun. Many of you already know. Many of you suspect and have not begun.

If you wish to investigate the form of expression that would be most appropriate to your own inner self, before you go to sleep at night, write your question on your tablet or in your journal. Ask: "What form of expression is most in harmony with my inner self?". When you awaken, the very first thing in the morning, notice what answer is in your head. Ask the question again and notice the answer. Recall your dream. Write down a brief note on your dream. It is possible that you would have had a dream seeing yourself in the form of expression most in harmony with your inner self. It may be something you haven't ever thought of. It may be that your most natural harmonic form of expression is as an ~~airline stewardess~~ FLIGHT ATTENDANT, simply sharing yourself with others. It may be that your most natural form of expression of your own Isness is as a mediator in business. Any skill, any talent can be used to express yourself, and in expressing yourself, experience your connection to your brothers and sisters, experience your connection to the universal, to God.

There is no hierarchy in forms of expression. To dance in a majestic ballet is equal to building a perfect birdcage. It is only the ego that ranks forms of expression as better or worse than other forms of expression.

Children, particularly those under ten, if they have been left to their own development without much intrusion, are spontaneous expressers of their own aliveness. Children have a great deal to contribute to adults. Children are in tune, for the most part, with their connection to God. If that connection has not been intruded upon by violence from the outside world (violence including hunger and disease) the child will naturally express joy and celebration. Before the age of, approximately ten, most children are still free from the decisions that inhibit or restrain one's expression of Isness.

As children, each of you choosing to manifest yourself in human form experiences the unity, the celebration of life. However, even as children your own karmic patterns, your own individual memories were with you. It is out of these patterns that you chose your particular parents and circumstances. The patterns are reinforced by the circumstances you created for yourself. Some of you were more willing to experience joy than others. This is not good or bad. This is part of the program created in your karmic patterns.

CHAPTER SEVEN

Free will is a part of the human experience. Each time you come to a part of your pattern, you have the opportunity to exercise free will. Free will allows you to break the patterns in your individual karmic system. However, free will is influenced by the system. Over and over and over again, even though you have free will you choose to repeat the pattern.

(and overrides the option available to the free will. However, you do)
The ego has identified itself with the pattern. The ego fears death if a choice outside the pattern is made. The ego ties you to the pattern

have free will. That is to say, you have the ability to choose freely, to will your reality into existence consciously rather than unconsciously manifesting the patterns in your subconscious karmic system.

The use of affirmative statements is an attempt to exercise free will. The use of what is called "affirmations" is an attempt to override karmic patterns. This system is useful and can allow you to overcome karmic patterns. The fault with the system is that it is superimposed on the pattern. It is impressed upon the pattern. It is riding over the top of the pattern. Eventually affirmative statements can be used to break the patterns because you will be creating new patterns. When those new patterns have a strong enough identity of their own the old patterns that have preceded them will eventually disappear.

This system, however, requires much diligence because if the affirmative statements are discontinued the old, more familiar pattern, surfaces. Likewise, the new pattern can- not take effect until it has as much energy connected to it as the old pattern. Each pattern in your karmic system. through repetition, has an amount of energy connected to it. Each part of the pattern has a varying amount of energy holding it in place, so that, as few as twenty affirmative statements may be sufficient to break one link in the pattern. Two thousand may not be sufficient to break another link in the pattern.

Most systems that use affirmative statements suggest that the affirmative statements be made a particular number of times. However, if one is to use this system to break patterns. one must be open to one's own intuition or instincts as to the appropriate number of times to use the affirmative statement with each separate part of the pattern one is focusing on.

For those of you unassociated with the use of an affirmative statement to shift one's reality, we will explain. It is possible to notice the pattern of one's thought in a particular area. For example, one may notice that one has the thought, or a basic decision, associated with money, that says: "I am poor". If one notices that thought, one can reverse it. In the most simplistic form, one can say, "I am rich". The use of the affirmative statement, or affirmation is employed to reverse the thought patterns that one is creating one's reality out of.

It is a useful system. However, some patterns are more difficult to break than others. Therefore, a set number of times of repetition is insufficient for the variety of patterns existing.

Affirmative statements are useful to keep the conscious mind centered on a pattern that you wish to overcome. However, it is an overcoming rather than a breaking-up. It would be more expedient to break-up the pattern. Patterns have varying amounts of solidity within your karmic system. Therefore, the number of times you would need to repeat an affirmative statement varies with each pattern. Since you have no way of knowing the number of times such repetition would be needed, you have no way of knowing how long you need to focus, or how many times you need to repeat an affirmative statement to overcome a negative pattern. While the system works, it would be more expedient to use the dream state to break-up a pattern. However, the repetition of an affirmative statement allows your conscious mind to focus on destroying a pattern.

If you choose to use affirmative statements, or are accustomed to using affirmative statements, we suggest you combine it with the use of the karma-breaking technique earlier suggested for the dream state. Therefore, if you are, in the example previously given, repeating verbally, or writing repetitiously that you are rich, having discovered that you have a pattern that says you are poor, it is useful to combine the affirmative statement you are rich with the technique of writing on your bedside tablet or in your dream journal that you wish, or intend to break-up the pattern that says you are poor. You may combine these techniques.

It is useful to combine the techniques, because as you focus your conscious mind on the affirmative statement, you will begin to notice thought patterns that indicate you are breaking-up the pattern. However, simply over-riding the pattern is ultimately not as useful as erasing it. Therefore, if you use affirmative statements we suggest you combine it with other techniques designed to eliminate the pattern which produces the negative thought pattern.

Many other techniques beside the use of the dream state, are available at this time through various groups, workshops and disciplines. Some of these groups, or workshops, or trainings use a pattern-breaking technique based on the technology associated with the group labeled Dianetics. These techniques use a systematic peeling off of the layers associated with a pat-tern. That is to say, the pattern is identified and then in a written or verbally applied technique, layers of thought holding the pattern in place in the individual mental system, are systematically removed. This technique, to dissolve patterns is also useful.

To apply this technique yourself, to your own individual pattern, simply identify the pattern. Sit with a pen and a tablet and write the pattern at the top of the page. Then list the following items in regard to that pattern: First list the thoughts associated with the pattern. Then list the beliefs associated with the pattern. Then list the feelings or emotions associated with the pattern. Then list the decisions associated with the pattern. Then list ideas and body feelings associated with the pattern. For example: if the pattern is "I am poor", list the thoughts associated with being poor. You may notice you have the thought that you will always be poor. Or the thought that poor people will go to heaven. Or that it is good to be poor. Continue till all the thoughts are listed. Then list the beliefs. You may believe that it is more spiritual to be poor. Or that members of your family are always poor. Continue till all your beliefs are written down. This technique may also be done using a tape recorder.

When you have peeled off all the layers of thought associated with the patterns, the pattern will sometimes disappear. However, there are decisions holding the pattern in place in your subconscious mind as well as in your conscious mind. This technique removes the thoughts associated with the pattern in the conscious mind. It is a very useful technique. It allows the thoughts in the subconscious mind to be nearer the surface. Hence, once again we suggest the use of the dream state in combination with this conscious mental process.

Until the karmic pattern, lodged in the subconscious mind is erased or broken, the pattern will continue to manifest itself in your daily reality. However, removing the conscious mental decisions often supports removing those decisions which are subconscious, or part of the karmic pattern lodged in the subconscious.

Various other techniques are also available to you. Another technique frequently used by New Age workshops is the technique of visualization. This technique attempts to impress and alternate image on your subconscious mind. That is to say, one begins to create a mental picture of oneself freed from the limit of a negative or unwanted thought pattern. In the example given, one would begin to see oneself as rich. One would begin to see oneself surrounded by luxury. spending freely, having and doing all of the desired things.

This system is also useful because it begins to impose a pattern on the subconscious mind through the imaging. Pictures, visual creations, are more readily impressed upon the subconscious mind than are verbalizations. This is because the subconscious stores impressions that are at once visual, verbal and emotional. To create a mental picture of a desired behavior or situation one must mentally verbalize the picture. That is to say, you see yourself richly surrounded, spending money freely. Each thought used to delineate the picture is a verbalization. The picture is a visualization. Therefore you are combining these two aspects that are linking the pattern to your subconscious mind.

It is wise, in this technique to add emotion, or feeling, to the picture. So that as you are imaging a situation or a circumstance that is the one you desire to create for yourself, add feeling or emotion. In other words: see yourself richly surrounded, spending freely, and also feel as you think you would feel if you were doing that. This impresses the desired pattern on the subconscious more completely than merely imaging.

As you image, verbalize the image specifically and clearly. Add emotion or feeling to the image. Keep the image, the verbalization and the emotion consistent in using this technique. You may also want to use your dream state to transcend the pattern that you are using your imaging to reverse.

Creative imagery is also useful because it allows the conscious mind to begin to experience itself in a new reality. It also allows the conscious mind to begin to realize that that reality is created by your thought patterns. Thought patterns can be controlled and the resulting reality you create can be shaped consciously. Thought creates reality. The technique of creative visualization helps to allow you to experience consciously your ability to create your reality.

There are other techniques available to you in the game of disconnect-ing your real self from your karmic pattern. However, these techniques, mentioned above, are the most widely used and effective at this time.

CHAPTER EIGHT

In the beginning of your sojourn on Earth your human mind created a system of patterns that you have been operating out of in each subsequent lifetime. Each time you are reborn into a human form you carry the previous human life experiences with you into your new, or current lifetime. All those patterns that have contributed to your previous life experiences are lodged in your subconscious mind and your current reality is created by the thoughts associated with those patterns. Therefore, for you to transcend the system of duality on Earth, which has shaped all of those patterns you must take responsibility for their existence and eventually for their creation.

This book is being written to facilitate you in transcending those patterns. The techniques already mentioned are effective in assisting you to break those patterns. However, what must come first is the realization that you are not your patterns. You are not your mind. You are not your feelings. You are not your decisions. You hold all those elements within the truth of who you are. You are much greater than any pattern or system your mind has created. You can rise above those patterns and it is appropriate for you to do so if you are to discover your true identity. It is also imperative that you break negative patterns that tie you to the system of duality, of separateness, of good and evil now existing on Earth if you are to assist others and demonstrate to others that this can be done.

We, on the planet Venus, and many, many other physical and non-physical, are available to you to assist you in breaking or transcending those patterns which tie you to the system of duality. Each of you has several non-physical presences connected to your consciousness that are cheering you onward. These presences have been called by many names in many systems. In a religious context they have been called guardian angels or protective saints, or in Eastern philosophy they have been labeled as various gods and goddesses or keepers of realms of consciousness available to the advancing spiritual awareness of the individual. In metaphysics these presences are sometimes referred to as spiritual guides, or teachers, or ascended masters.

Children often experience the presence of their guardian angels or spiritual guides. Children can sometimes see or experience these presences. Adults frequently chide children for talking to so-called, "imaginary friends". These friends often are actually the non-physical presences associated with the consciousness manifesting itself as a child. Many of you may recall your own, so-called, "imaginary friends" when you were a child. Those presences were often really this. It is possible for you, as an adult, to regain contact with these non-physical friends.

Each of you has access to those consciousnesses that guide and assist you in your daily life and in your expansion of your awareness. Contacting them is easy and useful. It is also fun. They are wonderful playmates. They guide and assist you constantly. They have been with you always. They are your partners in your sojourn on Earth. You are the one who chose to manifest yourself in physical form. They chose to assist you and participate with you in the experiment of duality on Earth. They came when you came. They have been here as long as you have. They have been with you as long as you have had a physical form.

Some of these friends have, in one of your lifetimes or another, manifested themselves in physical form. Sometimes they chose to come and play with you in a body. Usually, however, they choose to remain in non-physical form. If they chose a physical manifestation, they did it to assist you and to have more direct physical contact with you. They are much less attached to physical reality than you are. However, many of them are also learning from you. As you grow and experience life in physical form they are with you. They learn with you. They expand with you. They grow with you. They are here, available to you now.

You can contact these non-physical friends in the following manner: After you have read these instructions, close your eyes. Take several deep, relaxing breaths, imagine yourself seated in a comfortable, large chair in a well lighted room with a door opposite you. When you have become very relaxed and very comfortable in that setting, ask that your guides to present themselves, one at a time, to you in that room. Ask that the door be opened. Ask and you shall receive them into your conscious presence. See the door opening. Allow whatever figure wishes to present itself to enter and stand before you. Do not concern yourself with their physical appearance. The physical attributes they present to you in this exercise are not important. They will, knowing your thought system, present themselves in a form compatible to your reality. You need not fear any evil or negative presence. If a form appears that discomforts you tell it to leave. You are in charge of your own reality. You create your own images. There is no evil outside your own system of duality. There is ultimately only goodness, only God, only pure energy. Any image that appears that is upsetting in any way is your creation and you can dismiss it simply by telling it to leave. You are the one creating your reality.

Even though you create your reality, the presences of other consciousnesses associated with your own consciousness, are valid and real. You attract to your self any negative image by your own negative thoughts. Do not therefore, feel any fear in using this technique, then you will not attract or create any negative image.

As you sit in your chair with the presence and the image of your spiritual guide before you, ask them if they have any message, anything they would like to tell you. Always, in receiving a message as in receiving any input in physical reality, trust yourself first. Know yourself, first. Be open to input and also use your own experience, your own judgement in receiving or acting upon any other input. These guides are here to assist you. They are available to your conscious mind in this manner. Other techniques for guide contact have been used in workshops and seminars associated with New Age thought. If you are accustomed to another technique and that technique works for you, continue to use it. Or, begin using it again if you have left off making contact with your spiritual advisors in this manner.

Using your spiritual guides, or non-physical friends, is a short-cut for contacting your own, so called, super-conscious. These guides are, in a sense, part of your own super-conscious mind. They are part of you. They are part of who you are. Though we speak of them as separate from you, they are so linked to your own consciousness, that they are actually a part of it, as are many other consciousnesses that may be co-existing with you in physical form. There is a network of consciousness that you are linked to that make up a sort of family tree of consciousness that eventually taps into the source of all energy. We will be discussing this family tree in this book.

You, who have chosen a human form to manifest your expression of the Isness, have many guides and teachers, both in physical and non-physical form. It is easy to recognize a teacher when you are playing the role of student in a classroom. Most of you have also recognized other human beings as teachers of a less formal nature. Many of you acknowledge the role of your brothers and sisters in human form who have taught you lessons on your journey through this lifetime. Some of those teachers were your parents. Some of those teachers were your friends. Some of those teachers were religious or philosophical leaders. You have learned from books. You have learned from your actions. You have learned from observing the actions of others.

There are among you also non-physical teachers and guides or facilitators. These non-physical guides also learn from you. They have attached themselves to your consciousness in order to contribute to you and to learn through you. These guides are in no way negative. They are there to assist you in your growth and spiritual development. They are available to you. They enjoy being used. They appreciate the opportunity to interact with you on a more conscious level. They constantly interact with you on a super-conscious level. They are with you in the dream state. They have access to your subconscious mind and can support you in completing your karmic patterns in the dream state. They do this.

In addition to the personal guides which are ultimately facets of your own super-conscious mind, there are also masters or teachers associated with various aspects of development. If you are a musician, there are teachers and masters associated with the field of music. These teachers are available to you as you perform or practice your music. There are specific masters and teachers available to those of you who express yourselves through the written word. There are masters and teachers for every aspect of human growth and development.

Some of these teachers were once in human form. That is to say, the energy which once manifested itself as a human form is still collected and identifiable with the personality and the talent which once expressed itself in a human body. These are not ghosts. They are not discarnate souls wandering the wasteland of the astral plane. These are teachers existing in a non-physical realm who are available to you if you choose to allow them to contribute their gifts to you.

That is the way this book is being written. We on the planet Venus, though never having appeared in a dense physical body on Earth, are familiar enough with the human mind and the human situation on Earth, that we can relate to you from our perspective. Because we are not attached to the human drama, we can see what is happening more objectively than those of you acting out the drama. Hence, our point of view is useful to you in disconnecting yourself from the drama and realizing more completely the fullness of who you are.

In addition to those guides and teachers mentioned above, there are other non-physical consciousnesses available to you. You are part of a huge network, a family, literally a family tree, manifesting your root of consciousness through many branches. Some disciplines and information available on Earth discuss the concept of, what has been called, an Oversoul. An Oversoul energy is what it seems to imply. It is an energy that is over many consciousnesses at the same time. However, once again, since time is an illusion it is difficult for the conscious human, everyday mind to grasp the reality of the Oversoul network.

Imagine a bush with many branches. Imagine that bush has several roots underground, all connecting to a main tap root that reaches deep into the Earth. Take the image of that bush with that root system and turn it upside down. Imagine that the tap root reaches upward into pure consciousness, into the light, into what is called God. Imagine the associated roots as parts of the same consciousness existing in non-physical form. You may call them angels. You may call them guides. You may call them higher energies. By higher we mean closer in awareness, in consciousness to ultimate consciousness.

Those of you who have thought or have been told that you are higher or more spiritually advanced. sometimes referred to as an "old soul", are actually not higher in any hierarchical sense of the word. All that means is that at some level you are more conscious and more aware of your connection to ultimate consciousness. It means that in this lifetime or in previous life experiences, you opened your awareness to truth to a degree beyond that of the level of awareness generally associated with human form. It does not mean that you are better. or more elevated. It is a grave mistake to use an acknowledgement of your level of awareness as food for the ego. That is diametrically opposed to truth. As you become more aware of your true identity, you become less separate. To use any information to separate yourself, or place yourself above your brothers and sisters is a distortion of truth. It is a delusion. Hence, your non-physical guides, teachers, and masters, while existing in an arena of consciousness that is closer to the source of ultimate consciousness, are not better than you. They learn from you as you learn from them. Your interaction with them is of benefit to all.

Back to the bush. Imagine then, that the branches of the bush which, if it were not inverted, would be above ground, are the portions of the whole manifesting in physical form. The bush has many branches. They are all part of the whole. Some of the branches have many smaller limbs, each connected in a dendritic pattern, all leading eventually to the tap root which connects to God consciousness. As you open your awareness you include more of the bush. You include non-physical presences and you can also include other physical presences on your particular branch. Eventually, as your awareness opens in its fulness, you will include the entire bush as you.

In the beginning you chose what form of the Isness you would manifest. You have chosen many, many times. Each time that you make a new choice, there are new experiences for you. Each time you chose a particular form of manifestation new areas of the Isness are available for you to experience. This time you have chosen a physical, human form. At other times, particularly before you chose to manifest yourself physically on the Earth, you existed in varying degrees of physicalness.

Some of you had more experiences in dense physical bodies than others of you. There is no hierarchy in this. An angel of the highest frequency is as much part of the Isness as is a stone. The only difference is the form of manifestation. However, the angel is more aware of its connection to the ultimate Isness than is the stone. Therefore, the angel has more fun. It is more conscious. It knows. It creates. It plays in the vast potential of the Isness more easily than does the stone. However, both are merely reflections of the Isness. The angel is not better. The angel is simply more aware.

The vibrational difference between an angel and a stone is linked to the difference in awareness. As one gets more conscious of one's connection to ultimate Isness, one's vibration rises. That is why it has been so difficult for some of you to be here on the planet Earth. When you left a higher vibration, a higher frequency of energy than is current on Earth, or indeed was current on Earth, for the Earth has, despite appearances, raised its vibration since the beginning. When you came to Earth your vibration was lowered, your vibration became dense physical matter. In the mechanics of lowering your vibration you lost some of your awareness of your connection to God. The loss had an effect on you. It still does.

Each of you shut down some of your awareness in the transition into your dense, physical, human body. The game on Earth has been to remember where you came from. The game has been to raise your vibration. The game has been to regain your connection to all that is. You, reading this book, are winning the game or you wouldn't be reading this book. Each of you carries within you the memory of "home". Each of you at some level, recalls the light. Each of you, whether consciously or unconsciously longs to return. Each of you wants to be with God.

Each of you has a family tree. Each of your con- sciousnesses is connected to a line of other conscious- nesses. Some of these consciousnesses are manifesting themselves in physical form at this moment and others are not. Time is an illusion. Time ultimately does not exist. Therefore, any other consciousness in your lineage that chose to manifest itself in physical form is manifesting itself right now. However, within the illusion of chronological time, that other consciousness in the lineage of your consciousness, that is to say, that branch of the consciousness that you share, that chose to manifest itself in a different aspect of the illusion of time, is co-existing with your present reality. That is why you have the ability to tap in to that other time and place in the lineage of your own consciousness.

You may tune in to other aspects of your con- sciousness' experience through various so-called, remembering or regression techniques. These techniques assume the illusion of chronological time. Chronological time is a device for the human mind to be able to order and delineate experiences within physical form. Physical form needs a past, present and future in order to experience itself persisting. Therefore. time is attached to physical form. Those aspects of your consciousness that did not choose to manifest themselves in physical form exist beyond the illusion of time.

Those parts of the lineage of your consciousness that did not choose physical form, that exist in non-physical reality are present and available to your human consciousness at all times as they exist beyond time. Therefore, they are in that sense, always present with you. You may communicate with them at any time and experience their presence. As part of the lineage of your consciousness, they are attached, or associated with your consciousness. They are on your pathway back to the source of all energy, of all consciousness. Existing beyond the illusions of time, form, and distance, they are more aware of the truth of their connection to ultimate Isness, to God. In that awareness they are able to share an overview with you that, should you choose to use it, can contribute to your own awareness and expand your experience of your own connection to God. Those aspects of the lineage of your consciousness have been called guardian angels. They have been called spiritual guides. They are available to you.

It is easy to contact those aspects of your consciousness that are existing in non-physical forms. It is useful to contact them as they can speed up the expansion of your awareness. In speeding up the expansion of your awareness, they contribute to the more rapid elimination of the system of dualism. They exist outside of the system of dualism. They exist outside of the illusion of evil. Therefore, they can contribute to your awareness from a perspective that is not generally available to you in the consciousness of the everyday human mind.

Many great artists, many great philosophers, many great musicians, many great scientists, many great mathematicians, many people throughout what is called history, have used their connection with these non-physical aspects of the lineage of their consciousness to bring forth creations beyond the normally anticipated creations of their day. Many breakthroughs in science, in mathematics, in the arts have been received by individuals who are open to the non-physical presences sometimes called muses, which are associated with their consciousness.

The muses are also available to you. You can open your awareness to them and allow them to channel information and ideas to you that are out-side of the usual thought patterns locked into your own human consciousness. They can feed you information and ideas that are not associated with your own karmic-mental patterns. That is the main benefit of opening up to those levels of awareness associated with the non-physical aspects of your consciousness. They can give you ideas that do not logically follow from the karmic patterns which create most of your daily thoughts. They are beyond ego. They are beyond the illusion of separateness. They wish to and enjoy contributing to you.

Contacting your own muse, your own non-physical consciousness, your own guide or guardian angel or teachers on other levels of
consciousness is easy. It is available to you. Various techniques have
been brought forward in various disciplines and religions. Many
times people who feel that someone speaks to them in their prayers or
in their so-called "musing", are actually hearing aspects of their own
consciousness. Sometimes this is called the higher consciousness.
They are not higher in any "better than" sense. They are simply more
aware of their connection to ultimate Isness and are not bound by the
ego to separateness.

To contact your own muses use the technique mentioned earlier of
sitting in the room and inviting them to present themselves through
the door and come into your room. If this technique does not work at
first, continue to use it and as you use it notice any other thoughts or
feelings or emotions that come into your awareness as you practice
this technique. If other thoughts or feelings come up, just look at
them, ask that thought or that feeling what there is for you to learn
from it. When you know what there is to learn from it then let it go
and focus on the technique again. If you continue, eventually, other
thoughts which have been wanting your attention, other feelings that
have been trying to express themselves will eventually be completed
and the technique will reveal to you your guides, your muses, your
angels.

When you do contact them it is wise to treat them with respect, to
acknowledge them, to thank them. You may ask them how they would
like to interact with you and when they would like you to contact them
and how they would like you to contact them. Always, you should
weigh their advice, however, for the most part we suggest you are
open to it. If you ever have any question about the advice given, that

is to say if you ever feel there is any negativity in the advice given, simply ask the one who gave the advice if this advice represents the consciousness of the highest good of the light. If you have a Christian background, you may ask if this advice or direction represents Christ consciousness. If it does not, the one giving the advice will disappear. The trick is to trust yourself. They are aspects of yourself. We invite you to trust them and trust your own experience as well.

CHAPTER NINE

In the beginning of your sojourn on the planet Earth you became a human being. You set aside your link with the consciousness you experienced being a part of before you came to Earth. This link still exists. You can open your awareness to experience that connection once again. Earth is moving rapidly toward the completion of the experiment in duality. You are a part of that completion. You have manifested yourself on Earth at this time to be present and contribute to the completion of evil in the human system. It is a choice you made eons ago when you first chose to come to Earth. You would not be reading this unless you were part of the consciousness that chose to participate in the completion of duality. Your part in the plan was written long ago. It is now time for you to recall your mission. You have something to contribute to your brothers and sisters as we all, collectively, move toward the completion of the experiment in duality.

You can discover your mission. You can remember why you chose originally to come to this planet. You are part of the plan. You have had many lifetimes on Earth, but Earth is not your home. You left your home when you came into physical form. Your home is with God.

Many of you have locked within your memory banks, remembrances of experiences on other planets, in other dimensions and in other realities than the reality your human mind is familiar with. These memories create in you a deep-seated awareness that life can be different. That life can be joyous. That life can be a celebration without pain, without suffering, with-out fear. You know that the negative experiences you and others on Earth have and have had are not necessary to life. You know another way. That is part of the frustration you feel as you hear of the suffering, past and present, on your planet. You know that it is an addition. It is imposed upon truth. It is not the way it can be.

You are here to shift the planet away from the creation of evil and suffering. Each time that you, however slightly, participate in creating suffering for yourself or another you know you have missed the mark. The word sin in ancient Greek meant to miss the mark. Sin is not bad. It simply is not the truth. Throughout history punishment has been associated with sin. Punishment also misses the mark. Punishment perpetuates sin. They are the same as they are not based on truth. Joy, delight, celebration are truth. You are all that there is. Everything is you. Every act you perform toward or against another is an act toward or against yourself. At some level of your awareness, you know this. You experience pain when you create pain. The pain you experience is the knowledge that you have missed the mark of truth in your action or in your thought. You are not separate from your brothers and sisters and all other forms of life. They are you just as the body you inhabit is you. There is nothing in creation that is not you.

Devils and demons are you just as angels and gods are you. All is part of the creation we collectively, brought forth. However, it is now time for aspects of that creation to disappear, to dissolve, to fold in on itself and leave no duality. Evil can now fold in on itself and disclose the truth that pain and suffering are not needed to experience God. God is all there is. You are a part of God and at the same time, you reflect other parts of God in the perfect Isness.

Evil was created by us all. Evil exists on Earth because we chose to experience the system of duality. Duality is based on the false premise that there is something other than you. Evil is based on the illusion of separateness. You are ultimately not separate from any thing or anyone. You are part of all that is. You are connected to all that is. Each time you have a thought that sees another as not you, as not a reflection of you in one of your many facets, you perpetuate the illusion of separateness. Likewise. each time you relate to another with love and compassion and rejoice in their unique expression of God, you create unity. you hit the mark, you bring forth the experience of truth.

We. collectively. in all dimensions, originally chose to split off from the one, from the source of all energy. to experience ourselves, to know that we are God. We chose to discover our ability to create. In that process of discovery we created the experiment in good and evil. We created duality. We have learned and experienced all that is necessary in that experiment. Earth herself has experienced the range of evil and good and she is ready to complete the experiment.

This book is intended to allow you to begin to lift the veil from your own consciousness. For many of you the memory of what it was like where you were before you came to Earth is so painful in contrast to your experience on this planet that you have buried it deep within you. Yet you know that at some hidden level you have the knowledge that the experience of life can be much different than is presently being manifested on Earth and you long to go home.

For many of you the experience of your personal connection to God is so painful because it is associated with the sense of having lost or left behind that connection. In that case you seemingly prefer not to experience that connection here because it is so lacking in comparison to your previous, though hidden, experience. Uncovering your connection to God is what this book is about. It is imperative that you rediscover your personal connection to the Isness if you are to participate in the end of duality on this planet. Your connection to the Isness is absolute. You are a part of the Isness at the same time as you are a reflection of the Isness. That Isness is called 'God'. That Isness is all that there is. A system of duality being experimented with is a part of the Isness. It is time for that part of the Isness to complete itself. You are here. You are reading the book, this book, because you are part of that completion.

CHAPTER TEN

The Isness exists in perfect unity. Separateness is an illusion. You have been participating in the illusion of separateness. It is time for you to discover and express your true identity. You came to Earth many, many lifetimes ago. When you first arrived the circumstances on Earth were vastly different than those you had experienced at home. You made many decisions about what it was like to be a human being. You made many decisions about what it was like to be on Earth. Those decisions have kept you from experiencing the memory of your home. Those decisions have, in some cases, kept you from experiencing your connection, your true connection to God.

Many of you have been able to conceptualize your relationship to God. Many of you have been able to accept the theory that God exists and you have been able to relate to that theory, however, many of you have not truly, and deeply and completely experienced your participation in the Isness, your connection, your link to God on a personal level. You are connected to God beyond all circumstances, beyond all forms, beyond time.

If you were to know yourself fully, you would know yourself as God. You would know yourself as part of All That Is. God exists in you and expresses through you because you are a spark of the Isness. You are a reflection of All That Is.

To experience oneself as unified with all life is to know oneself, is to lift the veil from the illusion of separateness. As you use your dreams to break your attachment to your physical body, you will be disconnecting from the illusion of form. As you begin to develop your relationship with your personal spiritual guides, with that aspect of your own Higher Consciousness which they represent, you will be experiencing your connection to God. As you begin to break those karmic patterns within you that are based on fear, division and separateness, you will discover your own unity with All That Is.

Another technique for lifting the veil from the illusion of separateness is the technique called past-life regressions. Once again we use the word 'past' only because we are speaking in the illusion of time. All of your life-times actually exist simultaneously. All of the people or animals that your consciousness has expressed itself through or has manifested, are existing, right now, if we remove the illusion of time. Time and space are illusions, however since you chose to experience form, time and space are needed for you to allow form to persist. So we will use the illusion of time to speak of previous life experiences. We will speak as if chronological time exists. Ultimately it does not.

When you first chose to manifest yourself in physical form on planet Earth, it was, however much the experience had been previously described to you, a shock. Form on earth exists at a much lower vibration than form does in most of the experiences you had previous to incarnating on Earth. This lower vibration helped to close down your memory of the previous experience. Existing in a dense physical form was very different than existing in a less dense, less defined form.

You made certain decisions about that experience that initiated your karmic patterns. Many of you thought that you had made a mistake. Many of you regretted leaving the higher vibration because in that higher vibration you were more aware of your connection to

God. Rediscovering that connection has been part of the test, part of the game you assigned to yourself in coming to Earth. Perfect Isness exists everywhere in everything including you. You on the planet Earth have chosen to participate in the game of duality. Duality is a system in which opposites appear to be necessary, in which opposition appears to be necessary. Conflict is not evil. Evil is the apparency of separateness. Earth is not separate from God. You are not separate from others. Others exist with you in the heart of God. All of us collectively are reflections of the multi-faceted potential of the Isness.

In the beginning of your sojourn on Earth decisions you made began creating your point of view. The vibration on Earth was a shock to many of you who had existed in a less solid or higher frequency vibration. Where you cam from is not better than Earth. It is all God, all part of the Isness.

However, where you came from was outside of this particular experiment in duality. Therefore you know that life can be expressed without evil. Therefore when you confront evil in yourself, that is to say, the illusion of separateness within yourself or within your brothers and sisters or the society of which you are a part, or as you observe other societies on the face of the planet, you grieve. There is a sense deep within you that life need not be this way. That violence need not exist. That suffering need not exist. That deprivation, either physical, spiritual, psychological or emotional need not exist. When you find yourself participating in any form of suffering, either personal or sociological, at some level you grieve. You long for the end of suffering. You want to reconnect with God. You know that that connection can be real in your experience.

Many of you have participated in various forms of religion or other so-called spiritual disciplines, or searched through various philosophies to regain your own personal experience of your connection to what is called God. You have been searching because, at some level, however deeply buried within you, however covered with karmic patterns and decisions, you know that it is possible. You remember.

Many of you have had brief moments of experiencing that connection to God. Some of you have had charismatic or mystical experiences of unity. You may call it the experience, in the Christian tradition, of being saved. Many of you have used drugs of one form or another to break out of the prison or your mental structures and experience a reality beyond that which normally encases your experience. Many of you have had transcendent moments in experiencing art, or music, or dance, or poetry, or drama, in which you, however briefly, reach into the core of your being and experience yourself as greater, or more than you normally experience yourself. You have experienced moments of connection to your brothers and your sisters in romantic moments or in what has been labeled, "peak experiences".

The experiences of transcendence of individual separateness are familiar to you when you are having them. That familiarity comes from your own pre-Earth experience. You know that this is possible. You long to experience these moments. These moments are food for your soul. These moments are frequently what makes life worth living. You seek these moments. You seek them in your relationships with others. You seek them through your work. You seek them through your religion. You seek them because you know they are there. You know what it can be like to experience life as joyous, as connected, as one with something or someone beyond the shell, or limitation of your own ego.

The ego is threatened by these moments of transcendence. The ego is threatened by any loss of separateness. The ego's job is to keep you identifying with your individual mental structures, with your individual patterns, with your experience of isolation. That is why you experience difficulty in attempting to transcend your own isolation. When you reach out to another in total compassion and experience them as you, your ego is threatened. When you transcend your karmic patterns and experience your unity with All That Is, the ego is threatened. When you reach beyond yourself through art, through philosophy, through the experience of union of any kind, with that which is without your own limiting mental system, your ego is threatened. It is the job of the ego to keep you separate. The ego identifies with the individual human mind. The ego sees its survival as dependent upon continuing to create the illusion of separateness. It is time for the ego to die. It is time for the ego to disappear. It is time for separateness to be ended. If the experiment in duality is to be completed on Earth, the illusion of individual separateness must end. This is a threat to your ego.

The ego can be befriended. The ego can be tamed. You can treat your ego as a friend. It has been your friend. It has given you, through eons of time, the experience of duality. Through the experience of duality you have participated in the illusion of good and evil. You have experienced facets of the Isness that you would not have experienced without the existence of the ego. The ego has contributed to your wisdom. The ego has shown you what it is like to experience yourself as separate, as distinct. The ego has created opposition and in that opposition you have learned much.

You know what pleases you. You know what displeases you. You know joy and you know sorrow. It is time to let go of sorrow, both on an individual level and on a societal level. Ego has served its purpose. We all owe ego a debt of gratitude. Ego has not been a villain. Ego has not made us victims. Ego is. Ego is a part of the Isness created by all of us in order to experience duality. Ego has served its function. We created ego for the purpose it has served. It is now time for us to transcend our own creation.

You may interact with your ego as if it was a friend. You may ask your ego what it needs to allow you to move forward in your experience of unity with All That Is. You can tame your ego as you would tame a pet. You can give your ego a name. You can take your ego out to lunch or for a walk in the park. You can feed your ego with attention and with your own friendship. Your ego is a part of you, but it is not you. You have, within the illusion of separateness, identified yourself with your ego. You have thought that your ego was you instead of knowing that the ego was a part of the system of duality. As such it is something that you have, just as you have thoughts and feelings. Your thoughts are not you. Your feelings are not you. They are things that you have. They are actually things that you create. Your ego is part of your creation. Your ego did not create you — you created it. The ego is there to be transcended. It is part of the plan that the ego dies to itself. It is part of the plan that the ego be dissolved. It is part of the plan that the function of the ego which created the illusion of separateness be completed.

We suggest that you begin taming your ego. We suggest that you sit quietly, in a safe location, close your eyes and introduce yourself to your ego. Ask your ego its name. Ask your ego what it wants. Ask your ego how you can make it comfortable as you begin to transcend the illusion of separateness. Your ego has been reading this book with you. You ego knows what you are up to. Your ego will feel threatened.

It is feeling threatened right now. Console your ego. Let it know that it is a part of you, and that as such you cherish it as you cherish all that is you.

Ask your ego what it needs from you in order to be your partner in your commitment to transcend your own separateness. Ask your ego to be your friend. Bargain with your ego until it feels safe enough to work with you in your quest for unity, rather than against who you truly are. Tell your ego that the game of duality is coming to a close. Tell your ego that you want it as an ally. Tell your ego, you are the one in charge of your reality and that you now chose to move toward the pole called God. Ask it to assist you. Ask it what it needs to be your partner. Your ego is ultimately your creation and you are in charge.

You are a spark of consciousness connected to many other sparks of consciousness. Some of these consciousnesses are manifesting themselves in physical form. Some are not. You are connected to the consciousness of every, so-called, previous life experience that you have had. You are also connected to those non-physical consciousnesses associated with your consciousness, earlier referred to as spiritual guides or guardian angels. Ultimately you are linked to all other consciousnesses and to ultimate consciousness. Your own lineage of consciousness includes all of your, so-called, past-lives. Decisions that you made in any of those previous life experiences are still a part of your own subconscious mental system. Therefore when you first incarnated in physical form on the planet Earth, the decisions that you made are still a part of your mental system. Those of you coming from a vibration in which physical form was less dense than it is on the planet Earth, lost contact with the higher vibratory consciousnesses associated with your own consciousness. This is an opportunity for you to regain that connection. This is an opportunity for you to, once again, contact that level of awareness which you shared before you created your human form.

Some of you existed in physical form on other planets, or in other dimensions of an equally dense vibration. Therefore the shift to human form was not as much of a shock to you. Those of you who came from a higher vibratory level felt the loss of your connection and have grieved. You have at some, deep subconscious level, longed to return, longed to go home. Like E.T. you have wanted to "phone home". This is an opportunity for you to do that.

The guide meditation, mentioned earlier, is an example of how you can contact your own Higher Consciousness. In the same way you can also contact those consciousnesses associated with the dimension and location you existed in before coming to Earth. As you are sitting in that meditation, in your room, comfortably relaxed, ask that your teacher from your home appear to you. Your home may be a planet. That is to say, it may have some physical form in some dimension or it may be that you associate home with the flow of energy existing in what is called space and not necessarily attached to a particular planet. Hence, the teacher that responds to your request, may or may not appear in physical form. If it does not appear in physical form it will present itself as consciousness or as light. You can interact with this consciousness in the same way that you interacted with your spiritual guides. As you sit in the meditation you can ask that representative associated with what you call home to take you back with them to the experience of home. That experience is still available to you. It was never lost. It was only the shift in vibration that made you think that you had lost that connection. It is available to you.

In the meditation when you go home, your own vibration may raise. Your own level of awareness may expand. Relax into that expansion. Allow the limits of your conscious mind to fall away and allow your awareness to spread out into infinity. That experience is within you. When you are in the experience of home, look back at your present life. Give yourself any message about your current condition, situation or relationships. Ask yourself questions. Answer them. In that higher vibration, in that expanded awareness, you can be your own teacher. You can be your own spiritual guide.

It may take a few sessions of practice before you are able to relax enough to allow yourself that experience. Continue the sessions until you are able to return home in your experience. When you have experienced being home notice, in that experience, your connection to what you call God. Notice your relationship with the light. Notice your connection to ultimate Isness, to pure energy. Allow yourself to revel in that experience. That is the truth of who you are.

When you are in that experience, recall what you were first told about the planet Earth. Go to the point in that experience when you were first told about Earth. Notice what was communicated to you. Notice what was asked of you. Notice what you were told. Look and see if you had a purpose in coming to Earth. Look and see what your mission was. Look and see what you were told about the beings, or people on Earth. What were you told about their needs? What were you told about their awareness? What were you told about the crisis, or shift that would take place on Earth? Hear the answers clearly. Remember them. Then use that information to evaluate your current occupation, your current relationships, your current activities and interactions on Earth.

You have a purpose in being here. You are part of the plan. You are part of the shift away from the pole called evil. You have been here long enough to participate in evil — to experience the infliction and creation of evil and to experience its effects. What you need to do now is to rise above the decisions in your mental system, in your memory bank, that tie you to the thought that evil is necessary, that suffering is predictable.

These exercises in expanding your consciousness beyond Earth, beyond your human form, will allow you to experience the existence of life beyond the system of good and evil. These experiences will allow you to know that you do not need a devil to experience a God. These experiences will allow you to return to your own awareness of your capacity for joy, celebration and union.

CHAPTER ELEVEN

Your consciousness is linked to a family of other consciousnesses. Many of these consciousnesses are currently manifesting themselves in physical form on Earth. Your family may not be the physical family you were born into. Many of you have already discovered your own spiritual, or artistic, or creative family. You chose your parents to complete certain karmic patterns. You chose your parents, in some cases, simply because they were vehicles available for you to bring your consciousness forth on Earth at a particular time.

The astrological moment in which you chose to be born is an important tool that you created, or used, to trigger certain karmic patterns within your system so that you could complete them. Sometimes you chose your parents simply because they would allow you to be born at the precise moment that would allow the energies of the planets to trigger patterns within your system that you wish to complete this lifetime.

You use the stars. They do not use you. You are not their victim. You are their creator. You aligned yourself with their energy so that the influence they brought to bear on your human consciousness would be consistent with those tasks you set up for this lifetime. You can use your astrological chart to give your conscious mind clues as to what patterns you chose to complete in your current life experience. The patterns were there, latent within your mental system. The stars did not create the pattern. You use the stars to trigger the patterns so that you can complete them.

There are forces in the universe which are as natural a part of creation as is your human body. These forces are also consciousness. These forces exist in nature. These forces effect and are effected by the flow of consciousness as your own consciousness is and does. These forces exist everywhere and effect everything. Your own consciousness can effect these forces and they can effect you. The science of astrology deals with the forces of the planets upon consciousness.

Astrological forces are not the only forces in nature which effect your consciousness. In addition to the effect on your individual consciousness of your previous life experiences, the influence of your spiritual guides and teachers, the astrological effects of the planets on both your birth and your daily life, there are other forces in nature which are part of the flow of consciousness you exist in. These forces effect your energy. These forces effect your thoughts and your feelings. These forces surround you. The most obvious invisible force that effects you is gravity. Gravity holds you to the Earth.

There are other forces besides gravity that also effect your consciousness. You are not the victim of any of these forces. They are part of the game you created. The trick is to work in harmony with them. The trick is to hold them. The trick is to not work against them.

There are locations on the planet of very high energy, places where the cloud of duality is thin. These places energize you. These places are locations where the Earth breathes, where the Earth's energy is released. When you are in one of these locations you feel energized. Likewise there are locations where the Earth breathes in. In these locations your consciousness feels sucked down.

Each location has a specific vibration as each location is a part of consciousness. Just as you, as an individual, resonate at a certain vibration, so do physical locations. When you are working on any of the techniques mentioned in this book we suggest that you find a location that resonates in harmony with your vibration. There are places in your home where you feel more comfortable than others. Take time to find these locations. You may need to change the arrangement of the furniture in your home to make it comfortable for you to sit in a location where you feel energized and awake. As you become more awake and aware you may even, in time, choose to change your residence. Where you live has an effect on your consciousness. The items you surround yourself with have an effect on your consciousness.

If you have surrounded yourself with memorabilia from your personal past, you are less likely to move forward rapidly. Some items from the past may inspire you. Keep them. Other items from your past may hold memories or trigger emotions that depress you. Get rid of them. Let go of the negativity of the past. Clean your home. Make the place you live a place where you feel energized and alive. Surround yourself with things that inspire you, that bring you joy. It would be better to live in an empty room, one that you can fill with your own consciousness, than to live surrounded by items that, however slightly, depress you.

Set up a plan to go through your home. Set up a plan to go through your office or your desk where you work and your car and any other physical location where you spend time. In each of these locations, allow yourself to focus for a moment on each item that surrounds you. Ask yourself what thought, or emotion, or feeling that item brings up in you. If you are inspired, or uplifted, or cheered by an item keep it.

If an item is neutral and useful in a practical sense and forwards you in making your life easier, or your job more efficient, keep it. Clean it. Make it appealing to the eye.

However, if an item, however useful in a practical sense, depresses you or reminds you of a negative experience, or connects you to a person with whom you feel some animosity or estrangement — get rid of it. Clean up the place you spend your time. Make a list of items you want or need to make a particular location more compatible with a positive attitude and an efficient method of functioning. It would be better to do without items you wish to have than to have around you items that weigh down your consciousness.

This exercise will also demonstrate to you that you create your environment. That is to say, you create your reality. Each time you eliminate an object that weighs down your consciousness you free yourself. You create the opportunity to fill a part of your consciousness with joy instead of filling it with negativity of any kind. It is important to keep the areas you inhabit clean and orderly. This frees your conscious mind for creative activity. It is better to simplify your environment than to keep it cluttered. As your environment is cluttered, so is your consciousness.

As you go through each location where you spend time, ask yourself how you feel there. Ask yourself what you could do, what you could change, in order to make yourself feel more comfortable, more alive, more inspired in that location. Then do it. It may be, that as you chose to remove items from your environment, you realize there are incompletions in your life. You may have books on your shelf that belong to another. Return them. You may find things that are broken. Repair them, or throw them away. You may find letters

that are unanswered. Answer them. You may find projects that you
began and never finished. If these projects inspire you and give you
joy, complete them. If they do not give them to someone they would
inspire and have them complete them. Otherwise, get rid of them.

You may need to make a list of communications to deliver to
people in your life. You may find things around you, items in your
environment that you never fully appreciated or acknowledged.
Write on your list to thank your mother for the socks she sent you, or
your father for teaching you how to wire your stereo. You may find
negative things that need to be communicated in order for you to free-
up areas of your consciousness. You may need to acknowledge
birthdays or anniversaries that you had forgotten. You may need to
acknowledge items that you stole. You may need to pay debts or bills
that you had overlooked. Make a list of these items and systematically
deliver the communications. Handle each item. As you do, you are
freeing up space in your consciousness for creativity and joy. Completing old projects, either by finishing them or discarding them,
creates space for new projects, new ideas, new creativity to flow in.

Look carefully at the area of money. Money is energy. It is
symbolic of the flow of give and take between humans. If there are
areas of the flow that are blocked, you are blocking the flow of money
in your life. Make a list of debts to be paid. If you cannot pay those
debts now, communicate with the one the debt is owed to and make
an arrangement by when the debt will be paid. Then keep your
promise. If you are unable to keep it, communicate with them and
remake the promise. Keep it clean.

It could be that you have silently promised yourself something.
You may have promised yourself a new muffler for your car, a facial,

a new dress, a vacation — include yourself on the list of people you owe. If there is something you no longer desire, acknowledge it and eliminate it from your list and from your consciousness. If you promised yourself to quit smoking: quit. If you promised yourself to start exercising: start. If you promised yourself a day in the mountains: take a day in the mountains, or schedule a day in the mountains that is convenient for you. Or, if you find you no longer want to go and spend a day in the mountains, then release yourself from that promise.

Make a list of things for your car, either maintance, repair, or improvement. Then begin scratching each item off of your list as it is complete. Make a list of areas of your health that you have been promising yourself to handle. Make the dental appointment. Have your eyes checked. Update your insurance. Once again look at this area in terms of maintenance, repair and improvement. Do those things you have been wanting to do. See a nutritionist. Get a pedicure. Whatever it is for you. List it and begin scheduling time and money to complete each item on your list.

It is not selfish to take care of yourself. As you clean up your environment, your body, your relationships, you are creating space, you are freeing yourself by freeing your consciousness. You are opening the doorway for creativity to flow into your life. You are releasing yourself so that you can move forward with your mission on the planet. You are cleaning up your life so that you may more fully contribute to others and also experience joy.

You, as a spark of light are pure consciousness. It is easier for you to know yourself when the space around you is uncluttered, when your relationships are whole. We, on the planet Venus, applaud your courage. It is not easy to begin to accept the truth of who you are. As you become yourself, you will be stepping outside of society's normal point-of-view. You will be experiencing yourself far beyond the self which you presently are identifying with. Who you are is much greater than this. Who you are is a spark of God reflecting and expressing God, surrounded by parts of yourself.

CHAPTER TWELVE

The word metaphysics means beyond physics — beyond those things which are physical. Each of you is a metaphysical being. Each of you goes far beyond your physical reality. Using your dreams to astral travel, to complete karma, is one way of coming to know the possibilities within yourself. Connecting with your spiritual guides, with your "home" planet, with your own Higher Consciousness, is another way to come to know the greater you.

An additional way to get to know your true self is through past-life regression. Once again, we use the framework of chronological time for the simplicity of discussion. Ultimately, all of your life experiences are taking place at this moment. You are, at this moment, in this body reading this book. You are at the same time existing in other dimensions, other physical realities and in other human bodies. That is to say, your consciousness — that branch of consciousness that you are a part of — that comes directly from the source of all energy, or from God, is manifesting itself in several physical forms at this moment.

Within the framework of chronological time you have lived many other lifetimes on Earth and before Earth. For the most part, lifetimes in other dimensions or on other planets, outside of chronological Earth time, are of no major significance because lifetimes vary. Some consciousnesses never experience death, or shifting of physical vehicles.

You are existing in this body and in the body of every other lifetime in your experience at this moment. That is why in a regression you can experience the emotions and the thoughts of your other self. Sometimes the experience in a regression is more removed. You are more of an observer than a participant in the experience. That is accurate. You are the observer of all of your experience. You are even the observer of this current experience. You have been playing dress-ups. You have been masquerading. You have been pretending to be various human beings in human forms in different time periods on Earth. Each of these experiences was designed by you, for you.

Each lifetime that you have experienced was created by you for a specific set of reasons. Unfortunately, many of these reasons were based on karmic patterns which evolved from the decisions you made in previous experiences.

When you first arrived on Earth you began making decisions. You decided what it was like to be a human being. You made many decisions about other human beings — male and female. In each previous life experience you made additional decisions. All of those decisions have interwoven to form a karmic pattern. You have made choices based on illusions. Those choices have brought you to where you are now. Those choices have colored the point-of-view through which you're reading these words.

You chose each of your previous life experiences in order to know yourself more fully. You have experienced good and evil within the system of duality on Earth. That was your choice. Each time you chose to experience a situation that could be called evil, either as the receiver or as the giver, you did so to more fully participate in the potential of the Isness. It is now time to stop creating circumstances that could be categorized under the pole named evil. The Earth has had enough of such experiences. You have had enough of such experiences. It is time to end suffering. It is time to cease experiencing pain and fear and loneliness. These experiences were part of the game. These experiences were constructed by all of us so that we might more fully know the potential of All That Is. Now it is time to move on.

However, each time you experienced a situation that could be labeled negative, you made decisions. Those decisions tie you to the pattern associated with good and evil. That is to say, each time you experienced something painful, you, at a mental level, decided you would never do that again. For example, part of your mission on Earth may be to lead others. However, it could be that you, at some point in the history of your previous life experiences, created a situation in which you were put to death because you were a leader. That is to say, you created a circumstance in which your death was associated with the fact that you were a leader. Being a leader does not kill one. Being a leader is being a leader. However, for reasons of your own, you may have used your position of leadership to end a particular lifetime. If that is the case, you probably made decisions at the time of your death about leadership. You may have decided, for example, that being a leader is dangerous. You may have decided never to be a leader again. You may have developed thoughts, ideas, beliefs, emotions and decisions about being a leader. When you are in the drama of a particular lifetime, you are not consciously aware that you created the dream. You are not consciously aware that that lifetime is a game you are playing within an illusion.

The illusion of separateness allows for a game to be played in which it appears that there are antagonists and protagonists, in which there is opposition. It is the nature of most games that there are winners and losers. Sometimes you chose to lose the game. However, when you did that, you did it only to experience what it was like to lose. Unfortunately, when one is in the game, or in the drama, one forgets that he chose the game. Winning and losing is taken seriously. Winning and losing is made real. It is not. It is all part of the game within the illusion of separateness.

If, in the example given above, you decided to never again be a leader, that decision is part of the mental system existing within the karmic patterns of your subconscious mind. In this life experience it may be imperative that you become a leader. It may be your mission on Earth, at the time of the shift, to lead others or to be an example to others. If you have a decision in your mental system to never lead again, you will experience resistance to your mission. That is why we advise you to use the dream state to break karmic patterns. You may also use the technique of past-life regression to break karmic patterns.

Past-life regression, at its best, allows you to unravel karmic patterns. When you go back, in your subconscious mind and discover a previous life experience in which you made decisions that are effecting your current life experience, you can eliminate the source of those decisions. You can discover that you created the dream. You have always been the one in charge of your experience. However, when you are caught in the illusion of the drama of a particular lifetime you forget that you created the dream. The dreamer forgets that he is dreaming. The dreamer takes the dream as reality. You have dreamed many, many dreams on Earth.

Each dream you created, each drama you constructed, each game you chose to play, you chose freely. However, if one made the decision that leadership was dangerous, one would create a reality in which leadership is dangerous. Hence, if that is part of your pattern, in this lifetime, when you approach a position of leadership, you will probably experience opposition. The opposition is present because your belief that leadership is dangerous is present. The opposition is not inherent in the act of leadership. It is your beliefs that create your reality. Each time you made a decision in a previous life experience, you created a belief. You subsequently create your reality out of those beliefs. Sometimes you call it learning. Actually, it is limiting. You limit your experience of your reality with your beliefs.

Within the illusion of physical reality you have played many games. In these games you made many decisions. That is the job of the conscious mind. The conscious mind operates in a system of cause and effect. It is the conscious mind's job to sort out reality. In doing so it allows you to continue your physical existence. It is the conscious mind that reminds you not to step in front of a moving car. It is the conscious mind that reminds you that swallowing glass is dangerous. It is the conscious mind's job to sort out reality and guide you through physical reality. Unfortunately, however, some of the decisions made by the conscious mind are stored in the subconscious. This is not bad. It is part of the system generated to insure physical survival.

For example, in a previous life experience you may have accidentally ingested poisonous mushrooms. You may have become wretchedly ill. You may even have died. In this lifetime you may not enjoy eating mushrooms of any kind. You know that the mushrooms served to you in the restaurant are not poisonous. However, at the time the conscious mind made a decision that mushrooms were dangerous, that decision was stored in the subconscious mind. That decision is still with you. That decision still effects you. Hence, in this lifetime, seated in a pleasant restaurant, you may experience an aversion to mushrooms. At one time, within the illusion of physical reality, it was perhaps appropriate not to eat certain mushrooms. However, the subconscious mind does not discriminate. The subconscious mind treats mushrooms, to use this example, as a class of things. Hence, all mushrooms become dangerous.

The mind generalizes. Your mind generalizes. This is part of the system that has allowed for physical survival. It is part of the system that has allowed generation after generation to survive and evolve. It is time for you to take responsibility for this mechanism within the system of your own mental structure. The decisions are not bad. However, the beliefs, even if once appropriate, or seemingly appropriate, need to be transcended for you to move forward with your mission on this planet.

When you first left the ball of energy that we are referring to as God, you did not have a human mind. Your consciousness was aware of who you were and where you came from. However, in choosing to come to Earth, you also chose to be human. Being human includes having a human mind. The mind is necessary for survival of the physical body. However, you have identified with your mind. You think your mind is who you are. You are not your mind. You are not your body. You are not your thoughts or your feelings. Who you are is far vaster than any of these elements which you hold in the broader identity of who you are.

When your human mind began making decisions out of your life experiences of Earth, you began forming patterns of thought. Thought creates reality. You have been creating each reality you have experienced out of the patterns woven from the decisions you have made in previous life experiences. You have associated yourself, mistakenly, with these patterns. You are not the patterns in your subconscious mind. You can rise above them. You can break them. You can transcend them and discover your true identity.

As you look at your life notice any area where you are not fully joyous. Notice any limit that exists in your experience. Notice any relation-ship that is not fully loving. Each of these less than joyous areas represent or are manifested by thought patterns in your mental system that have been based on decisions from the so-called past.

As we have stated you can use the dream state to break karmic patterns. This is an efficient system. However, past-life regression is a quicker method to break or transcend karmic patterns. Past-life regression has been generally applied through a facilitator. However, this is not necessary. You can regress yourself to your own experience of your own previous lifetimes. The method to do this is simple. However, what is required is a very open attitude. As you begin to practice the following technique you will probably have many doubts. You may feel that you are not being successful. You may feel that you are making up the stories or experiences that are apparently previous lifetime experiences. Just practice. Just trust. Previous life experiences, like dreams, are stored in the subconscious mind. The response that your subconscious mind gives to the following technique will be appropriate. Trust your own subconscious mind. Allow the thoughts to flow. Give yourself permission to go wherever your thoughts take you. This is an adventure.

To recall, or experience your own previous lifetimes, you must first find an explicit limit, or feeling, or attitude, or thought that you wish to transcend. For example, in your daily life you may notice that you become very nervous when in a crowded elevator or in a small area of any kind where you are surrounded by many people. It may be standing in a line or in a large event. This nervousness could be defined as a fear of crowded places. It could be a fear of small places. Look at the fear and decide which is true for you. If you decide that the fear is associated with small, crowded places, then make a mental note of that fear. Use that fear as the basis of a private past-life regression.

Sometimes past-life experiences can be very emotional. Give yourself permission to experience the emotions that may be associated with a particular previous lifetime experience. To do this you will want to provide yourself with a safe arena in which to experience the regression. However, you need also to know that there is nothing that you cannot look at. Any previous life experience can be viewed by your conscious mind with objectivity. So that as you are re-experiencing a previous life experience, if the events you are experiencing become overly emotional or uncomfortably frightening, remove yourself from the experience by telling yourself that you are now going to view the experience from a distance. Tell yourself that you will now become the observer. Allow the experience to run-by your conscious mind as if you were watching a movie rather than as if you were acting out the drama.

After you have selected a thought pattern that you wish to transcend and have prepared a safe location where you can practice this technique uninterrupted, write down the fear or the pattern in a journal. You may wish to keep a record of the experience by using a tape recorder and verbalizing the experience into a tape recorder as you have the experience. That is recommended, however, it is not necessary. You will want to practice this technique in a location where you can lie down and be comfortable. When you are clear on the thought pattern you wish to transcend and have yourself situated in a location where you need not fear intrusion and where you can comfortably relax you are ready to begin.

Lie down. Take several deep breaths and allow your body to relax. Beginning with your toes, as you are breathing deeply, relaxing more and more with each breath, starting at your toes systematically move up your body consciously relaxing each set of muscles as you move up your body. In other words, you will begin by relaxing your toes. Then you will consciously relax the muscles of your feet. Then you will consciously relax the joint of your ankle. Then you will consciously relax the long muscles of your calves, etc. until you have moved up to the top of your head and have allowed your body to become very relaxed. This will allow your attention to be removed from your present life experience.

Then, when your body is relaxed, recall the thought pattern that you wish to transcend. Repeat it over to yourself in your mind. Then call on your guides. Ask your guides to take you to the previous life experience where you made a decision that established that particular thought pattern. Ask them to take you to the source of that thought pattern. Then watch the images that begin to come up in your mind.

Once you begin to get some images, tell yourself that you now want to find yourself in that story. Locate yourself in the story. To do that look down at your feet. Then look at your body in the story. Notice who you are. Ask yourself your name. Ask yourself the date and location. Take whatever your subconscious mind gives you and let the experience flow. Do not be concerned if the name that you get belongs to an historical figure or someone you have known about. The experience may not be literally accurate.

However, there is a reason why your subconscious mind is giving you this particular experience. So, accept the gift. Allow it to flow. Let it take you where it will.

Once you have located yourself in the story, begin noticing the facts of the story. Take yourself to your tenth birthday. Notice your situation, your family, your attitudes. From your tenth birthday, move yourself consciously forward to an event in that lifetime that has a significance for your current life experience. When you are in that event, begin asking yourself: "What did I decide?". Then ask yourself: "What else did I decide?" Continue asking yourself that question until there are no more decisions apparent. Then move yourself to the next significant event in that lifetime. Again, ask yourself what you decided. Continue in that fashion until you move to the event of your death in that lifetime. Notice the circumstances of your death. Then notice exactly when you decided to die. Notice who was in charge.

Ask yourself what decisions you made at the end of that lifetime. Continue until all the decisions have been pulled out of the subconscious mind. Some decisions may begin with the phrase: "I will never...". Other decisions may begin with the phrase: "I will always...". Additional decisions may begin with the phrase: "Next time I will do...such and such..." or next time I won't do...such and such". Notice these decisions. Notice particularly the decisions that have an emotional charge on them. As you do this exercise, notice how those decisions effect your current life experience. When you have completely moved through a particular lifetime, you may also wish to ask yourself, who in that lifetime is around you in your current life experience. Then notice how those relationships in your current life experience were effected or shaped by the previous experience.

When you have completed looking at a particular life experience, and discovering the decisions that you made in that life experience, move through the death of that body and notice any additional decisions that you made. Then ask your guides and your own Higher Consciousness, why you created that particular lifetime. Ask your guides to tell you what lesson you were learning. Ask your guides to tell you what previous karma you were completing. Ask your guides to tell you why you chose those particular events. Then ask your guides what agreements you had made before you entered that particular lifetime. You may want to ask some of the characters from that particular drama how your actions served them. You may want to notice how their actions served you in your purpose for that life experience. You may feel that you need to complete a communication with them. You may need to express anger. You may need to ask forgiveness. You may need to tell them that despite the apparency, you love them. They may wish to tell you that they loved you. Be open to such communication and allow yourself to complete the experience of that lifetime.

When you begin this technique you may not have many images. You may only get a sense of what would be there if you had an image. For you the experience may be less visual than sensory. You may think, "I do not see anything, but if I did see something, I would see two washer women in France discussing what it is like to be a mother". You may then notice that your decisions about being a mother are related to that particular experience. Just allow whatever experience is there for you to flow.

As you practice the technique, it will become easier. The key, however, is to give yourself permission. If you feel you are making-it-up, that is fine. If you feel it is. "only your imagination", that is fine. Allow your subconscious to give you whatever gifts it wishes. Play with it as you would a game. Pretend you are going to the movies. Allow yourself to discover your own creativity. Some of the experiences may be verifiable, others are not. This is not important. What is important is to begin to unravel the thought patterns in your subconscious mind. This technique is effective for doing that. This technique will allow you to begin to manage your thought patterns, to transcend you karmic decisions and create this reality unfettered by the past.

CHAPTER THIRTEEN

Those patterns that are a part of your karmic system can be transcended. Your attachment to your history can be transcended. Your attachment to the illusion that you are housed in your physical body, can be expanded beyond. You are a spark of the eternal Isness. You are a reflection of God. As such, you are a demonstration to your brothers and sisters of goodness. You hold the potential within you to save the world.

By carefully demonstrating the potential for goodness within each of us you can show your brothers and your sisters who they really are. In each circumstance, in each situation in your life, you have the ability to demonstrate goodness. In each moment of your own inner life you have the ability to choose the pole called God. In each interaction that you have with your fellow human beings, you can demonstrate love. You can rise above any negativity in your karmic system. Any area in your personal point of view that does not demonstrate goodness, that does not demonstrate God, can be transcended. It is now time for you to transcend the evil within the mental system that has shaped your point-of-view.

Your point-of-view has been based on the illusion of duality. Your point of view has been grounded in the illusion of separateness. Like other human beings, you have come to see yourself as the one who inhabits your body. You have come to identify yourself with your thoughts, with your feelings, with your beliefs. If you are to fulfill your purpose in coming to the planet Earth, you must transcend these illusions. You must discover and then demonstrate your own true identity.

Each human being you encounter or interact with has lost himself to one extent or another, in the illusion as you have. Each of your brothers and sisters is lost and wants to go home. You have the opportunity and the privilege, and the responsibility to be one of the lightworkers on Earth. You come from beyond the system of duality. You have a true home outside of the system of good and evil.

Like all of your brothers and sisters, you are completing the illusion of duality. However, because you now know who you are, you have a responsibility to yourself and to your brothers and sisters, to begin to live out of the truth. You have the privilege of demonstrating that love can be present without hate. You have the opportunity to experience and express God without God's opposite. Your own ecstasy and joy and celebration of life can be, and will be a demonstration to those around you of the potential of humanity. Human beings can live joyfully on Earth. The Earth herself can be renewed. This planet has suffered enough.

Each day, from the moment you wake up, you have the opportunity to express truth, to express God. Each day you can demonstrate to those around you, and to yourself, that it is possible to live fully beyond the system of good and evil. Each day you can do something to break your attachment to separateness. Each day you can demonstrate unity and love to yourself and others. Each day, in some way, you can fulfill your mission on Earth.

In the beginning there was pure energy. That energy was at once everything and nothing. That energy can be referred to as God. In the beginning God spoke and in speaking brought forth all creation. You speak. Your thoughts are spoken. Your thoughts create. You are God of your universe, creating constantly with your thoughts. However, you are the one creating your thoughts. You have the ability to monitor your thoughts in such a way that what is created by them reflects who you really are.

You are more than your body. You are more than your feelings, more than your circumstances, ultimately more than your thoughts. You are actually more than you can currently hold within your thought system. You are beyond thought. Thought exists within the human mental system. Before you came to the dimension which holds Earth you knew more completely who you are. That is part of why you chose to manifest yourself in this dimension. Knowing who you are, you were able to choose to come and participate in the experiment of duality. Knowing who you are, you were able to come and experience the effects of that aspect of the Isness that manifested itself as what we have called evil.

Evil exists within the system of duality. Duality is a system created by human thought associated now, only with the planet Earth. Your own human thought is a minute fraction of who you are. That fraction of a percent of who you are has limited your experience of your reality. You have so identified yourself with that minute part of yourself that you think that is who you are. It is not. Who you are goes far beyond the system that holds the experiment in good and evil. Who you are will exist when evil is no more. Letting go of evil will not be your destruction. Letting go of evil will be your resurrection. By releasing yourself from the system of duality you will free yourself and those around you to discover, experience and express more and more or your true identity.

Letting go of evil is letting go of separateness. Letting go of evil is an expression of your willingness to take responsibility for the God within you. Letting go of thoughts, feelings, ideas, beliefs, that separate you from your true nature and from your brothers and sisters is your personal redemption. As you redeem yourself, that is, return to your true nature, you will redeem others. As you redeem yourself you will naturally express that true self to those around you. People learn by example. Your life is an example to those around you. The way that you live makes a difference. The words that you say make a difference. The thoughts that you cling to make a difference. You create each time you speak. You create each time you give your energy to a thought. Thoughts that do not serve your true intention can be dismissed. When you notice that you are clinging to a thought which causes you pain or which separates you from your brothers and sisters, let the thought go, release it. Imagine that you have a laser gun that shoots white light and zap it!

When you chose to come to Earth, you chose to bring your light — you chose to share your light. You came to this planet to experience humanness, to play the game of duality and, when the time came, to be a part of the completion of evil. Evil has been a part of your human experience. You are not bad. You are not wrong. You are certainly not evil. Evil is part of the experience humans have created on Earth. That experiment in duality which allowed humans and the Earth herself, and all nature to experience that part of the Isness which reverses life, which denies the true purpose of life, has come to the time of its completion. You are here to witness and to participate in the completion of pain, of suffering, of resistance, of the denial of who you really are. That time is upon us all.

We, on the planet Venus, are with you as you search for the truth of your identity. Millions and millions of other consciousnesses in physical and non-physical dimensions are with you, supporting you, cheering you onward. Their thought is united in bringing forth the end of duality throughout creation. It is time for you to join your thought to ours. It is time for you to complete and eliminate those patterns within your human mental system called karma which tie you to the thought of good and evil, reward and punishment, right and wrong.

As you discover and take responsibility for your true identity you will have no wish or need to perform any action which harms another or which harms your true self. As you own the truth of who you are you will have no need to cling to any thought that denies the truth of your union with All That Is. Who you are is a spark of light — a reflection of God — a manifestation of perfect Isness, existing for a brief flash in the system called time, in a human body having human thoughts, playing the game of duality on Earth. Earth is preparing for a shift. It is a shift in the game. You are part of the plan made before time. You are part of the plan to end evil, to complete the experiment in duality. It is time for you to bring forth your part in that plan.

We recommend that you begin now, to consciously let go of those thoughts and actions that are based on the illusion of separateness The techniques mentioned in this book will assist you. Play with them. They are gifts you have given yourself to support yourself in your own intention to complete the evil within you. As you let go of those thoughts that separate you from your brothers and sisters, your actions will ripple-out and effect many. Your consciousness will join the millions of other consciousnesses which are holding the truth of who you are and which have already disassociated themselves from the game of duality.

As you expand your awareness of who you are you bring light to the planet. As you release the cloud of good versus evil from your own consciousness, your light shines brighter. Your light will bring light to others. As you release yourself from your own clinging to evil, the truth of who you are will shine into the hearts of those around you and they will discover themselves. You are a Lightworker. We, from beyond, salute you.

Rhea Powers and her husband, Gawain, live and work in Europe, the U. S. and South America. They lead seminars and conferences on the expanded, sacred and mystical aspects of life. For further information about their work please write to:

Rhea Powers & Gawain
P. O. Box 6456
Santa Fe, NM, 87502